Harness the Power of the Light

The Keys to

Psychic Protection

Teri Van Horn

Copyright © 2012 Teri Van Horn

All rights reserved.

ISBN-13: 978-1479301836
ISBN-10: 1479301833

DEDICATION

This book is dedicated to my clients – to all those wonderful people who have shared their lives, their energy, and their stories with me. This is for the ones who taught me to believe in myself and showed me that even the little things that I do each and every day positively affect the lives of others. We are all one!

My prayer is that in sharing this information, I'll be able to help even more people make positive improvements in their lives – just as they have positively impacted me and my life.

Blessings to you, my friends!

CONTENTS

1	Why do we need psychic protection?	1
2	What are psychic attacks?	8
3	Is this for real?	34
4	What is psychic protection?	60
5	Visualizations for Protection	64
6	The Power of Thought	69
7	Personal Psychic Shields	78
8	Shielding – The Why's & How's?	98
9	Additional Methods of Protection	105
10	The Power of the Spoken Word	115
11	Meeting Your Guides & Protectors	123
12	Protecting Your Space	141
13	Ways to Prevent or Stop an Attack	152
14	Protective Herbs	164
15	Quick & Easy Protection	169
16	Basic Spell-Crafting for Protection	172

1

Why do we need psychic protection?

Psychic protection is a major topic these days, due to all the negativity that we have to deal with. 2012 brought in some tremendous energy, bringing us closer to enlightenment and Ascension… but the down side is that it also brought more negativity to light. There's always a balance - if there's a lot of Light – there's going to be an equal amount of darkness/negativity, until this is completely cleared-out and we fully engage in the Ascension process.

There are many ways or forms of psychic protection: Guardian Angels/Spirit Guides/Protectors, personal protection, crystals, spells, feng shui… the list can be endless. What's vitally important is that we adequately protect ourselves, but not cross boundaries while we're doing it. We need to clearly understand what a psychic attack actually is and how best to clear and protect us, our home and our family.

It's vitally important that we harness the power of the Light to bring protection – particularly if we feel that there is a threat of negativity coming our direction. Light will always overcome the darkness, but you need to know what to do and how to use it to protect yourself from harm.

Some believe that the darkness is man-made, simply a figment of our imagination. Based on my experiences it's a little of both… there are negative energies and entities out there, as well as a lot of people who would like to do any of us harm. My belief is that through working with the Light, we'll be able to block these evil intentions and eradicate these people from our lives. This is my mantra, Light will overcome the darkness. I live it every day, in working with others, as well as in my own life.

That's not to say that I'm constantly being psychically attacked… on the contrary, I rarely am now. But, when I go into town, visit the grocery store, stroll through the shops downtown, I'm meeting people who are dealing with their own issues. They've had an argument with someone or their day started off badly. They're carrying around that little cloud of darkness and, being an empath, I'll pick-up on their negative energy. When I have a healing session, I'm dealing with my client's energy, therefore mingling it with my own in an effort to scan and determine the source of their problem. This, too is a way that I could be affected by negative energy… if I didn't protect myself.

There are many ways that we can go about protecting our bodies, our energy fields, our homes, offices, families and pets. The ones that we discuss here are primarily about shielding yourself, but there are a few techniques discussed about preventing individuals from doing harm to you. Whatever methods you prefer to use, either those listed in this book or some you find elsewhere, remember the Laws of Karma, the Law of Return or the Rule of 3 if you choose to do something.

No matter what it is you do towards another person… it can and will come back to you.

Is this really important?

We spend half our lives physically protecting ourselves. When you left the house today, you locked the door and set the alarm. When you got in the car to leave, you buckled your seatbelt and the car doors automatically locked when the vehicle was in gear. When you arrived at your destination, you looked around to see what was going on before you got out of your car and you probably did the same thing when you entered the building you were going to. If it is an office building, there was either a security guard, cameras or both watching the lobby and you had to have a key to enter your office. This is just the first few hours of the day… when you think about it, you go through about a hundred security measures each day.

BUT... how often do you ensure that you're protected on a psychic level? Do you really need it? ABSOLUTELY! If you experience any of the following, you need psychic protection:

- ~ If you meditate to expand your consciousness or practice shamanic journeys.
- ~ If you are a therapist or healer and giving too much to your patients and clients – leaving you drained afterwards.
- ~ If you use guided imagery or self-hypnosis tapes.
- ~ If people naturally gravitate to you to discuss their problems.
- ~ If you suffer from nightmares or panic attacks.
- ~ If you suddenly become accident-prone or nothing is working in your life – everything you touch goes wrong.
- ~ If you begin experiencing spirits or entities around you that wish you harm.
- ~ If you feel out of control, ungrounded and invalid.
- ~ If you are continually tired, listless, overcome by powerful emotions – with a sense of invasion or wrongness?
- ~ If you notice or feel a presence 'watching' you.
- ~ If you feel a heaviness or fearfulness in a certain room in your home.

- If you sense a cold spot in a room or cold feeling on part of your physical body.
- If you feel someone touching you when you are alone or if no one is nearby.
- If you experience a burning sensation at the upper back, just below the nape of your neck, and in that area a feeling of 'entrance' as in energy going into your body there and burning the back of your heart chakra.
- Behavior and personality changes.
- Sudden onset migraines.
- A loss of self-esteem and/or self-confidence.
- Major changes in clarity of thinking or analytical ability.
- A drained feeling or fatigue without cause.
- Sudden weight gain without a medical explanation.
- Hearing harassment voices inside your mind, as in negative words, demoralizing and degrading you, and/or bossing you around.
- Illnesses that come on suddenly which doctors are unable to diagnose or that can't be explained.
- Sudden cravings for alcohol, cigarettes or drugs – particularly if this is something that you don't normally partake in.
- Hallucinations or hearing voices.
- Inability to sleep without having to take sleeping pills.

- Difficulty coping with everyday routine life – sudden inability to cope with responsibilities – things that were normally handled with ease.
- Sensing frightening shadows from the corner of your eyes, passing by a window or doorway.
- Depression without understanding or apparent cause; negative thoughts; feelings of sorrow or oppression.
- If you live in an area which contains high levels of noise pollution or congestion.

So much of the time these symptoms are misdiagnosed, and people are put on medication without even knowing the *source* of all their trouble. What I want to address is the issue of being drained psychically, physically and emotionally by someone else. There are indeed various ways a person can be psychically attacked: It can be just from their conversational contact with you with their complaints about something ongoing and you've not been able to make any progress with them in correcting any of their problems, hence feeling frustrated and drained emotionally from the contact. It can be from a negative spirit or negative energy wavelength residing in your home, a haunting. It can be from a negative spirit trying to attach themselves to you due to some sort of either failure on your part to keep yourself out of the lower wavelengths due to alcoholism or narcotic dependency and this is allowed because of a life lesson being given you. It can be from a spirit attached to you now due to negative Karma from a past life affecting your current life, (as in "what goes around is now coming back around"). It can also be from the situation of another person being involved in something of the dark: (i.e. witchcraft, voodoo, psychic warfare as a form of entertainment, fascination with the dark and involving themselves in dark subjects, negative video games, etc.) attracting those in spirit on the lower planes. Like attracts like. Even if someone is dabbling with something they are ignorant of or don't fully understand the ramifications and are doing something negative involving the contact of the Spirit Realm (i.e. the Ouija Board, negativity-based Internet forums, psychic warfare groups, etc.), there can be psychic attacks stemming from these associations.

If any of these situations or symptoms have come up in your life, you may need psychic protection. First of all, it is important for you to have any physical symptoms checked out and treated by a medical doctor. Although our belief is that many of these instances may involve negative energy, there are many times when it is necessary and prudent to receive traditional medical care.

2

What are psychic attacks?

A classic psychic attack is defined as the manipulation of supernatural energies and forces. Psychic attacks occur when negative energetic vibrations or frequencies are sent from one person to another – or from a person to an object representing the target person. This creates disturbances within the chakra system, which is considered to be the backbone of the human energy system. Our chakras regulate our energy exchange within our environment and once any type of energy infiltrates the chakra system (of an intended target) it will eventually morph into the physical body or the physical environment of that intended target. That's when we begin to see physical symptoms or illnesses develop.

Scientists have validated that everything that exists consists of energy representing itself in various vibrational frequencies – everything in the Universe is alive and has intelligence. These energies can be perceived or "further energized" with a positive or negative force. This then turns into a thought form to which we subconsciously attach a frequency via our unconscious mind, therefore causing a vibration to occur. The resulting vibration is then perceived (by humans) as being either negative or positive.

Our Universe is composed of diverse supernatural energies ranging from Angels and Spirit Guides to the mysterious and malevolent energies from the darker elements. Because of this diversity, it is critical to immediately verify where any approaching energy originated from by asking the question, "Are you from the Divine Light?" Pay attention to how you feel after asking this question. If you feel at ease, you are encountering a beneficial energy. If you don't… then you've encountered discordant negativity.

Once you're aware of the energy's origin, you can ask its purpose. Listen to your feelings, imagination and intuition for an answer to this question. If you feel comfortable – that's a positive sign. If you feel uncomfortable, ask the spirit/entity/energy to leave. Shout it out… "You are not welcome here, now leave! Get out!"

This sounds overly simplified, but it's an essential step to keeping your energy field clean and clear. It's also the first step in implementing your protection. According to Universal Law, spirit is not allowed to lie. That being said, some spirits are sent to test us and if we don't ask these questions, then they may feel that they've earned the right to infect us with their negative energies. Universal Law does not allow spirit to deceive us if we ask where they came from. But… be careful because spirits can and will deceive you, just as people do.

Psychic attack can be as complex as someone cursing you- using black magic or something similar - or as subtle as living with a spouse or other family member who is angry with you a lot.

Maybe you work with someone who doesn't like you. They may not be obvious about what they feel, but you 'know' that something is going on. Psychic attack is anything that interferes with and invades your subtle energy field.

How do psychic attacks happen?

Psychic attacks involve the manipulation and movement of various types of entities, dark energies and spirits. This negative energy is transmitted into someone's energy body – their chakras or aura – and then it gravitates to the physical body or the person's physical space. An example is if someone is envious of something you have. They may not wish you ill, but the act of coveting what someone else has sets up a matrix for negative energy. Other negative energies that have the need to experience what someone else has will be attracted to the unsuspecting person, which in turn, will hurt or damage them in some way. There's no way around it… your envious intentions toward that person put everything into motion that happens to that person.

There is negative energy that is intentionally sent to create destruction and injury. It's usually sent with the intent to have power over, manipulate or punish the intended victim. This process generally involves a ceremony, ritual, the use of mind control or occult powers – in any combination.

One of the most important things a person must understand about a psychic attack is also one of the hardest for many to face:

Each of us bears a share of responsibility for the psychic attack we receive.

Simply put: if you are under an attack from someone or something, it is because you have opened yourself up to it somehow.

Sometimes, there is an obvious reason for a situation to exist. In these cases, it is necessary for you to own your share of what is going on. When you do this, the energy behind the attack often reduces significantly.

It's similar to a situation where two people are arguing. If one is willing to say they are sorry for hurting the others' feelings, things will often calm down instead of escalate. When you admit you have some responsibility in a negative situation, it can often affect the outcome in a very healthy and positive way.

Anger towards a person leaves you open. If you are feeling attacked by someone, then you may also feel angry or resentful. If you are angry or resentful with someone, then admit it to yourself. There's no shame to that - it just makes you human. But it is also necessary to take steps to deal with your emotions. Doing these techniques will not stop a psychic attack if you are holding onto intense feelings towards 'the attacker.' There must be detachment from the person who you believe is attacking you. Fear, jealousy, hatred, resentment, lust... all of these emotions, and more, leave us wide open.

Facing how you feel about a person or situation is not easy; it takes a lifelong commitment to self-mastery. If you are willing to face how you feel and accept that this is where you are right now, then you can begin to move through it. I didn't say "like it," I said accept it. Changing how you feel begins with acceptance of yourself - and of the other person.

If you are unwilling to do this, or unable to do this, at this time, it will still benefit you to do these exercises. Sometimes the willingness to confront your share of a situation will come with time. Time can bring you some detachment and with it, clarity. These exercises will tend to promote that clarity. So don't despair or judge yourself. Keep working on it and ask for help from God and from your own Guardian Angel.

When there seems to be no logical reason why a person is angry with you or trying to harm you, then it is almost certainly coming from something that happened in a past life. This can be hard to understand, especially if you are in a great deal of distress. You feel victimized and picked on. Maybe this is true, for this moment in time, but if you begin to study past lives, the concept of victimization loses its meaning. Over many lifetimes, you have traded places as the "victim" and "victimizer" again and again.

If a problem stems from a past life, it is my experience that it will start to clear up fairly quickly when the life/lives are brought into the conscious mind. It is not necessary to believe that it is a past life. It is only necessary to look at the situation and relationship with the person, in terms of the information received.

Following is a list of the basic types of psychic attacks:

Mental Attacks- are carried out by spirits or people possessing the psychic ability of telepathy, mind reading, some forms of empathy and others of the like. These attacks can cause light headiness, nightmares, fainting, disillusions and confusion. The best way to block these types of attacks is to set up mental barriers and blocks.

Energy Attacks- are carried out by spirits, people that are psychic vampires, psychics possessing empathy of certain forms, Astral Projectors, or other abilities based on spirit energy. These attacks cause tiredness, nausea, headaches, weakness, fainting, sickness, and sometimes death. To block these attacks put psychic shields and barriers. These can be produced by prayer or religious items as long as the person believes that they will work.

Psychical Attacks- [Physical] are carried out by spirits, people that possess any of the kinetics, Astral Projector users, or others that can affect the psychical [physical] realm. These attacks can cause psychical [physical] damage such as bruises, cuts, broken bones and other such injuries and even death. These attacks can be blocked the same way as energy attacks, but more energy must be used.

Controlled Spirit Attacks - are attacks like the ones above that are carried out by spirits that are ordered to attack another person. These attacks occur when someone uses a spell, curse, summon, or makes a deal with the spirit. The magnitude of the attack depends on how much energy the caster uses or what the spirit gets in exchange. If the spirit doesn't get much in return a simple block or shield will block the attacking spirit. While if the spirit gets the caster's soul and something else of high value to the spirit, it will continue to attack the person. The only way to stop the spirit at this point is to put up shields, blocks, and rely on your Guardian Angel to fight it off or in some cases even receiving Divine Assistance.

Subtle psychic attacks

These are some of the little ways that we receive psychic attacks:

Negative Thoughts - Years of belittling remarks projected by your parents, peers or a spouse. Negative thoughts turn very quickly into **Negative Programming,** which will negate you from functioning fully and effectively. If someone hears something about themselves enough, they will begin to believe it. This is the foundation of mind control and brainwashing.

Aggressive Thoughts - Unable to control your focus and self thought when being pushed by strong, convincing and persuasive sales people.

Enslaving Thoughts - Irrational actions from psychic bondage leading the person in destroying his family and wealth.

Places Of Negative Energy Fields - Places like mega cities, bars and gaming casino carry aggressive and stressful radiation and unintentionally transmit negative energy. Have you ever noticed how anxious you feel in these places?

Curse or black magic spells - A curse resulted from a spell or prayer, imprecation or execration, or other imposition by magic or witchcraft, asking that natural force or lower spirit to bring misfortune to someone. Most people who look spells and curses up on the internet are beginners, it takes skill and practice to perfect the more potent spells. The rest of these guys are harmless.

Dolls and Pictures - Usage of dolls, pictures or clothing to create a strong etheric link towards the victim to inflict harm to the physical body. This is like the voodoo dolls or wax figures representing the intended victim.

Throwing Energy - If you are angry and feel like smacking someone, it's quite likely that a little piece of your energy will shoot off from your and smack them. Maybe it looks like an arrow, or a ball of fire, bolt of lightning… well, you get the idea. There are too many ways to ever list.

There is no good reason to throw energy, even if they do it to you first.

Every time you throw something, you are that much more open to getting attacked by someone else, or an entity, or depleted in some way. Eventually this WILL have physical consequences for you.

Someone cut you off in traffic? It's very common to react by throwing a little zinger at that rude person. Think you will teach them a lesson? Think again. They will feel it all right, but it won't teach them anything you wanted to teach them - and it will leave you open to having energy thrown at you.

NEVER throw energy at anyone. That is a Psychic Attack and has serious side effects and consequences for the person who does it. The point is to protect yourself and not to violate anyone else. Any time you use energy for your own selfish use, it is wrong and there will be serious consequences.

Negative energy

Negative energy – negative vibrations – dark energy – dark spirits – Satan – entities – these can all create vibrational and energetic disturbances with anyone that they intend to interact with.

Before you incarnated into this dimension, you decided exactly what you wanted to experience during this lifetime. You mapped it all out – and now you're playing it out. Once you incarnated here, you no longer had control of how each of the life lessons you chose would play out. Quite often what we perceive as being a negative event, is actually an important part in our 'agreed-upon' life plan. At other times, that negative event might just be a blessing in disguise, with something wonderful occurring as a result. Don't judge what happens to you and don't judge what happens to someone else, because you truly don't know the reasoning behind every situation.

As we go through our daily lives, we are constantly sending out energy. If we send out positive energy… positive energy will come back to us. If we choose to send out negative energy, are hateful, fearful, taking advantage of others or even feeling and expressing lack all of the time, we will reap the karma of the energy that we are sending out.

This is why it is so important to pay attention to our thought patterns. According to Tufts University, the average person thinks 60,000 thoughts a day… with over 95% of those being repeated day after day. 90% of those thoughts are negative! That's a LOT of garbage going on in our minds!

When you find yourself deeply rutted in negative thought patterns, forgive yourself, then make a conscious effort to shift your thought patterns toward the positive. Quite often when we get in these negative ruts, it's hard to get out because we're constantly sending out and receiving negativity. It's a vicious circle and only we have the power to break it and make a course correction. Once you do… things will begin to come around for you. This is where you get the opportunity to harness the Light and make it shine!

What is a psychic vampire?

Have you noticed how sometimes after meeting up with a person who is sad or depressed can leaving you feeling drained and tired? Have you ever ignored a phone call from a friend because you just "didn't have the energy"? Does the prospect of even saying hello to someone make you almost run away in fear?

If you said yes, you have been subjected to a psychic vampire attack. This is done without malice or bad intention as the person is usually mentally weak or sick.

On the physical plane, they are the people who leave you feeling drained, or with a headache after you leave them. Maybe they touch you a lot and it doesn't feel nice.

Touch can facilitate the sharing – or stealing – of energy.

It can be difficult to protect yourself from someone who is constantly touching you to drain your energy or to poke at you. It's similar when someone gets very close to you, invading your personal space. That's exactly what it can be – an invasion.

We all know someone who is so lonely that they don't want to let you off the phone, or to say goodbye. They are desperate to share energy with someone and if you won't share willingly, then they may try and take it.

These people place a drain on everyone they meet, and generally end-up loners because no one can physically be around them for any period of time. I have someone in my life like that. We've even talked about what she does, but it continues. I've tried to explain how she needs to control and boost her own energy, but she doesn't want to make the effort. Sometimes I just can't be around it or her and I hate that, but I need all my energy to function!

Vampiring is when your friend accesses an unconscious flow of energy coming from you, to balance the lack of energy they have. This experience will drain you significantly. You need quick psychic protection in these instances to regain your balance, your focus and your zest to avoid dwindling along with them.

In vice versa circumstances, there are times you felt better after relating your problems to a friend. You have unconsciously sucked some energy from him making you instantly feeling better, oscillating back into a positive mode.

Entities, Ghosts & Spirits

What about a Spirit who is causing you strife? A feeling or a presence there in your home that makes you feel sad, depressed, or any type of feeling that initiates a negative sensation? Those types of energies coming from a Spirit can cause the human being on Earth to feel sorrow, depression, anything similar to a "flu-like feeling" which is all of the dark.

Why or how does this happen? There are some who believe that there are those of the dark who are released systematically so that there is a balance of Good and Evil in the Universe, and there are times when the dark spirit shows progress and has earned a type of reward by being allowed to visit the Earth to travel. Why doesn't that visit get supervised? It might, but there again having the manpower it takes to monitor all the negative spirits in the realm would be a huge undertaking, and although some do get away with causing trouble, sooner or later they get noticed which then causes trouble both for themselves, plus the ones who are supposed to report on their activities. There are also entities that truly are not of sound mind, and they, too, have earned visiting rights to Earth. Quite often these spirits attach themselves to people, places or things and that's how we get 'hooked-up' with them.

Some people have had a disturbing paranormal experience that "sours" them on or frightens them from exploring their psychic and spiritual nature. When you work with some of the simple exercises we're recommending, you will begin to develop more assurance and confidence. Learning to work with the highest intent you are capable of, is the way to begin.

Ouija boards and automatic writing are two of the most widely discussed danger zones for people who are being haunted or attacked by entities or ghosts. Much of the information people wish to receive from these spirits starts out as information or gossip about other people. Using any kind of activity to spy on or pry into another person's life or space is unethical and against Spiritual Law. I suggest that most people stay away from them, just because they do not attract the highest spiritual energies or Beings.

IF one is grounded, clear, and asking for protection from God, there is probably little danger in these activities - that is IF you are not asking improper questions about other people to manipulate them or otherwise get the "upper hand."

Just remember, Angels and Ascended Masters will not come through a Ouija board. A spirit may claim to be an Angel, but ask yourself why would an Angel need to use a Ouija board? The spirits that work through them are, at best, dead people. They have only a little more information than they did when they were alive. If your "Aunt Pearl" was controlling and meddling in life, what has happened to change her after she passed? There are always bored spirits hanging around willing to play with you... there are always nasty spirits hanging around willing to play with you, too... Be cautious and think before you start.

Be definite and set your boundaries about what kind of Being you are willing to receive Guidance from. I am willing to work with only Angels, my Spirit Guides or Ascended Masters, period.

One of the most common messages that people will get from a spirit is this:

"You are a very evolved Soul. You are a spiritual Master."

If you are really evolved spiritually...if you are really a spiritual Master, then you will not need a spirit to tell you this!

Be VERY suspicious of anyone or anything that tells you something like this. They are lying to you and playing on your ego!

A true Master does not need to be told they are a Master AND a true Master will not tell someone else this.

When you are open to receive any kind of message from anything that is listening, you are setting yourself up to experience something unpleasant. Some people are excited to have anything weird or unusual happen. Perhaps they desperately want to believe that there is something - anything - that comes after this physical life. Anything dramatic and unexplainable that happens will be some kind of indication that life will go on after death. Unfortunately, when a disembodied spirit latches onto a living person, the results can be terrifying -- and hard to stop. I have met countless people who were fooling around with the occult and had persistent and terrifying experiences that went on for months or years, with no way to stop it. They usually come to someone like me as a last attempt to regain their sanity. Think about how awful it would be to have things happening to you like that-- but no one believes you.

We had a very unpleasant spirit in my home for almost a year. Things started slowly, then progressed in intensity. It seems that my deceased father-in-law wasn't pleased with the fact that I had divorced his son and met someone new. We were living in the home that my former husband and I had purchased.

Initially there would be the obligatory footsteps upstairs when no one else was home. One evening I heard the sound of sails as they are filled with wind (he used to own a large sailboat and we sailed often). One weekend, my daughter was with her father and my husband and I were sleeping in. Suddenly we heard my daughter's bedroom door slam, her horse figurines fell off the shelves on her wall, then the front door slammed. I had immediately gotten up to see what was going on, but no one was there. I called my daughter and she was just waking up at her dad's house.
Another time my stepsons were visiting and while they were watching a movie in their bedroom, kept hearing the computer keyboard,

clicking away. It was across the room from them and nothing was near it.

One day my husband and his son were making some repairs in the master bathroom, while my daughter and I were walking up the stairs. Suddenly we heard a loud crash and ran upstairs, just about the time my husband and his son were coming out of the master bath to see what had happened. Somehow, a very nice lamp had fallen off the center of a desk, in the master sitting area, and broke. The lamp was approximately 18" from the nearest edge and no one was closer than 20 feet from it when it fell.

These instances continued to increase in our home until I was afraid to live there, although I had owned the house for almost 14 years. We were in the process of looking for a home in the country, so once we found the one we wanted, I moved there and refused to go back into my house in the city. It took a year to sell, but my sweet understanding husband met the realtor and took care of business there because I was so afraid to be in the house alone. Once we moved out of the house, all the problems stopped.

On the other hand, I've also had visits from my deceased father and they've been very loving and protective experiences. A couple years ago I was facing a potential health crisis… I was about to undergo testing for breast cancer and was worried, just as every woman is when she hears that news.

I was meditating in my office that morning, within a circle of crystals, but just couldn't focus or clear my mind. I left the room and went about my daily activities. About two hours later, I walked back into my office and discovered that a silk tassel had fallen off of an antique buffet and into my circle of stones. That wouldn't have been a big deal, but it was tied in a knot, about six feet from the stones and no one had been in the house. As I was contemplating how this could have occurred, I received a sense that my father was with me, letting me know that everything was going to be ok... and it was! This was his little way of letting me know that he was near and still supporting me. Later when the tests came back, the doctors determined that there were no traces of cancer and I've been perfectly healthy and clear ever since. I also know that although he's a little quiet, my father is always around, just as he when he was on earth.

It is not necessary to be terrified of anything "unseen," or to become superstitious, but you do need to be cautious and respectful. Although some of the exercises that I am writing about may seem silly, try them anyway. In the world of the spirit, your thoughts and visualizations are powerful. Here in the Earth Plane it is "Thought, Action, Manifest." In other words, we have to work to get our paychecks - we can't just think the money into the bank.
On the Other Side, it is different. Over there, it is "Thought Manifest." The strongest and clearest intents create their own reality.

With that in mind, what can it hurt to be prudent? *What goes around, comes around.*

Opening Portals

There was a new age store where I would occasionally fill-in for the owners, when they decided to travel to distant psychic fairs. One weekend I was splitting the 'shop-sitting' duties with another practitioner. I came in on Sunday and the shop felt different – cold, strange, almost claustrophobic. I didn't know exactly what it was, but I knew for certain that something had gone on in that space recently.

The store was full, but very few people bought anything or stayed more than a few minutes. They appeared to feel just as restless as I did – for no obvious reason. A couple other practitioners came in, but left immediately after their appointments. No one was comfortable being in that shop. Later in the afternoon a friend stopped by and spent the remainder of the day with me, chatting about energy work, reiki, and crystals. We were enjoying our chance to chat without having to help customers, but we both kept seeing shadows and sensing something moving throughout the building. Occasionally the lights would flicker in the other rooms and the place still felt 'stuffy'. Neither one of us was comfortable being there that afternoon.

My friend and I closed the shop together… we both locked and checked each door, we both went through the entire building and turned out the lights. We stood together as I armed the security system, we walked outside, doubled-checked the locked doors – again, and went our separate ways.

The next morning I received a phone call from the shop owners. It seems that when they arrived at their business the next morning, the lights and stereo were on, the doors were unlocked and the alarm was off. It appeared as though someone had just walked-out of the store instead of meticulously locking-up the previous evening, although nothing appeared to be missing. I was shocked… I didn't know what to say. I knew what we had done the night before and explained everything, in detail, to the owners. They didn't say anything else about it, but I discovered a few days later that the same thing had happened to my co-worker when she opened the shop the previous Saturday morning. It was already wide-open.

I also discovered the reasoning behind the shadows, and all the paranormal activity… it seems that a couple of psychics were in the shop on Friday before and were playing around with portals. They had decided to open the portal to the Titanic that afternoon, then when spirits started flooding into the shop, they didn't know how to close the portal or what to do about the spirits. So… they just didn't say anything to anyone and let everyone else deal with the problems.

The moral of the story is to not open portals, particularly to tragic events like the Titanic. It might seem entertaining to you, but think of those poor confused souls… what you should be doing is showing them how to go through their transition process, not bringing them to another place and time to play with. Portals to other dimensions should be utilized only by very experienced Light Workers, Energy Practitioners or Shamans. Opening portals can bring in energies and entities that have no business on this planet and who can cause serious harm to others. Please leave the portals to the professionals who not only know what they're doing, they can deal with and guide lost spirits to where they need to be.

Séances

I remember as a kid we would hold séances trying to connect with ghosts or famous people from the past. Of course, nothing ever happened because it was a bunch of teenage girls giggling, being silly and not having the skills or intention to pull something like this off. But… there are times when people decide to hold séances in order to reach spirits who have crossed over.

Let's face it, there's always something interesting that we'd like to find out from our dear departed family members. I have a great aunt that I always found fascinating. She was born in the 1900's on a small farm in rural Texas, along with 9 brothers and sisters, my grandmother being the eldest. This aunt, Pearl, supposedly had a young man that she was in love with, but who had died tragically. As a result, Aunt Pearl spent her entire life alone and grieving for this young man. I can't remember her ever wearing anything except black. She lived on her own, had bought a house and set-up a hair salon in the back room. She crossed-over when I was young, but I remember that she had very long hair that was always braided into a bun. She was a very nice lady and always very sweet to me.

As I've grown older, I've become to admire the strength of this lovely woman. Think about it… she lived alone and carved her own way during a time when it wasn't popular for women to do such a thing. She bought her own little house, near downtown, to open her shop. All of this happened in the 1930's and 40's in a very small Texas town. I find that quite amazing that she was able to accomplish these things, in a time when women were wives and mothers – they certainly weren't encouraged to go out and support themselves.

So yes, I'd love to be able to connect with Aunt Pearl to learn about her life and her journey. She lived until her 80's, always a pillar of strength. I'd like to hear about what life was like living on the farm with all her siblings, my grandmother being the eldest. And yes, I'd like to know how the family reunion is going in heaven, once the entire family had crossed-over. I know that she's spoiling my father, her favorite nephew, and that she's enjoying being with her entire family again.

BUT… what happens to sweet Aunt Pearl when I hold a séance to reach her and my grandmother? I bring them back to the Earth plane, we talk, I get the info, then we're done. I've had my curiosity taken care of and have been thoroughly entertained for the evening, but what really happens to these lovely ladies after we're done? I'll get to go back home, but many spirits are unable to go back 'home' after they're called back to Earth. We brought them here and we need to gently guide them back home – but this generally doesn't happen in séances and the spirits are literally left hanging out.

As much as I'd love to reconnect with these two lovely women, and my father, I know that it's best to NOT call them back merely to entertain myself. It's much better and more important to allow them the freedom to come to us on their terms, so that they can return to their heavenly home once they've completed their task. When we 'force' them to return to our plane, it often causes them difficulties and confusion and I believe that this is not only unfair to them, but it can cause both of us Karmic harm. It's best to leave our loved ones where they are and be grateful for any messages they choose to send to us.

Attachments

"Attachments" are actually a dark spirit or spirits coming into ones auric field and directly influencing the individual in a negative way. This generally occurs when we are in a low energy state and our natural defenses are down. They can instantly trigger a headache or shivers to occur. They also can affect the emotions of the human being causing them to feel oppressed and then subsequently depressed, as the human being doesn't understand usually right off what is actually happening and thus attributes this sudden and often unexplainable change in emotions and feelings to something they themselves are creating within them. In other words they think that this downturn in their feelings is caused solely by themselves, not realizing that it is that they are being victimized by a dark spirit. So when the person thinks that it is their own feelings being upset and depressed, they feel even worse. Education and knowledge about the source of the problem helps initially, which allows the person to have more control over the situation. Sometimes it becomes like a private inner war, battling to have control over your own thoughts and feelings with someone you barely can see, yet can sense them and their negative words telepathically influencing you, upsetting you, and trying to control you.

It is in essence an attack of attempting to possess the human being, making them feel more and more pushed out of their own physical body, and even standing offside of themselves if it continues. That is why it is so very important to block these attacks and to be stalwart in your own rights to your own body and not to invite or otherwise draw into yourself these negative spirits. They might flatter you or tell you something like "you are special" or something to that effect. The ego can be one's own worst enemy in this respect.

The three most common places to pick up negative energy are hospitals, cemeteries and funerals. Hospitals are full of patients whose energy reserves have been depleted and are wide open to attracting negative energy. In addition to this, they are full of spirits that have crossed-over, and for whatever reason did not start their transition to the other side. Anyone working in or visiting a hospital on a regular basis should always carry a piece of hematite, black obsidian, Black Tourmaline or smoky quartz to protect them from these discarnate beings. When you're in these places, you need to gather your forces and be as strong as possible, because they can and will attach themselves to you and you'll be drained for days after you leave there.

Negative energy thrives anywhere where there are negative emotions and negative people… almost anywhere! You can be walking down the street where something negative has just occurred before you arrived. Because energy patterns are imprinted in time, space, objects and places you are virtually always at risk to pick up some unwanted energy. The same goes for going into stores, renting apartments, buying homes (especially foreclosures)… this list is endless.

Meditation alone is not going to alter this type of attack. Prayer to God and the Angels to intervene is the only way you can summon the aid you need. We, ourselves, can try our best to fight these attackers off, yet we get tired and drained from the fight and then when we are at our wits end and exhausted, that is when these negative spirits can keep at it with having more than one spirit doing the attacking, taking turns fighting with the human. That is often why there are "attachments" (Plural), which is much like a group or a gang that does these types of attacks, not just one single demonic being bothering someone. It usually is several negative spirits taking turns ganging up on the human being, which is why it is so important to get this resolved early on, and not think by dismissing it, it is going to go away. Only the Divine can intervene and end this type of attack, but you CAN prevent it before it starts.

3

Is this for real?

Many people believe that negative energies, entities and psychic attacks don't really exist and that they're a figment of our imagination. Stephen Hawking, the greatest quantum physicist of all times, has proven that everything in existence consists of some form of energy. It is our perception of that energy that dictates the manner in which the energy field will affect us.

There are and will always be people around us who do not have the highest good for others as their intention and will do anything they can to take advantage of others. A lot of people out there will take advantage of someone who is experiencing darkness or negative energy, charging obscene amounts of money to 'remove the curse', often telling the victim that they need to come back time and time again… creating a steady cash flow for the scammer. These are the people you want to stay FAR away from!

Most legitimate light and energy workers will help you remove the negative energies/entities, by doing the work and providing the client with the tools and techniques to keep the unwanted energies away. The tools and techniques that are listed below are excellent for protection, as well as removing negative energies from you, your aura, your home… wherever you need to cleanse and clear.

With the current economic and government instability, when people aren't living in their power – they're becoming fearful and focusing on negativity and jealousy. They are sending out a collective vibration of focused malicious destructive energy. Although many of them may want to make their lives better, they don't understand what this does on an energetic level. Everything they say or do that's negative is blocking the flow of positive energies and abundance. When they do this, they will block any and all of the good things that were on the way to them. I've seen this happen many times, people will ask and pray for assistance, then just when help is literally around the corner, they'll become frustrated and start going negative. Once that happens, they push all the good opportunities and potential away, so that they can continue to attract what they are sending out.

As long as we stay in the positive flow and keep a positive, optimistic outlook in thought, word and deed, and do the physical work to help make things happen… our lives will change for the better.

When people become afraid, angry or confused they often unconsciously intend or send harm to someone else in order to get what it is they desire. This happens when our belief system is based on taking things from others so we can be in a position of power. When we are vibrating in the frequency of forcing power over others, we are in reality living our lives in fear. Since love and fear cannot exist in the same space… what's going to prevail? The emotion you feed the most!

Problems and difficulties can and do happen as a result of intentional focused negative energy and psychic attacks. This is why it's so important to pay attention to the energy you are surrounding yourself with at any given time. Pay attention not only to your own thoughts, but the people you surround yourself with, the books or magazines you read, and the television shows and movies you watch. Anger, fear, hatred, violence… these aren't just make-believe… these are real energies and if you surround yourself with them all the time… you know what you're going to end up with!

When people start dabbling with energies and occult things that they're really not familiar with, they get themselves in trouble. This is how we have problems with spells, curses, negative energy 'balls'… all of these things negatively affect us and the people they are intended for. This is one instance when Karma is very quick, because you'll be negatively impacted yourself, if you choose to do something negative to another person.

I have been a victim of a strong negative energy attack – in fact I was completely blind-sided one time. I had just started working in a psychic shop and met a woman who was acting very strangely. I introduced myself to her and we carried on a conversation for a little while. She had just decided to give-up her office at this facility in order to go on a soul journey. She was telling me about how powerful she was and how she channeled a healing technique and was teaching other people how to use it. She told me that she 'saw' a problem with my solar plexus and placed her hand on my stomach. I couldn't help the feeling of "something just not right" and she sucked so much energy from me that I nearly passed out and had to sit down. I've never had this happen to me and didn't know what was going on because I am a very strong person energetically.

A few days later I was back at the shop, helping out while the owners were out away. I had agreed to open and run their shop for five days while they were out of town.

On my first day I was turning on the lights, opening the window blinds and preparing the shop to be opened. So far – so good. I'd remembered everything I was supposed to take care of (it was a LONG list) and had gone upstairs to the manager's office to retrieve the money for the cash drawer. On my way down the stairs, I suddenly felt a push against my back and fell down about four steps, severely tearing the ligaments and tendons in my knee and horribly bruising my ankle. I knew I hadn't tripped, because I'd had a two-story home for many years. I also knew that I wasn't alone in the building at that moment... there was something upstairs – a very negative energy and it wasn't very friendly towards me.

In spite of my injury, I ran the shop for the agreed time and discovered a few days later that the practitioner who had seemed a bit distant and strange, had previously officed at the top of those stairs. She ended her journey early, wanting to come back to the shop, but had been told that her space was filled by me.

It took six months for my knee to heal, in spite of seeing a local specialist who took care of athletes from several professional sports teams. I now believe that her intention was to 'run me off' with the injury so that she could reclaim her office. I have sense learned from several people that this woman is notorious for draining other people and will even pretend illnesses to have unwary energy workers provide her with the additional energy she desires. She is also infamous for throwing these negative energy balls to people, in an attempt to get whatever it is she wants. I was a ready victim for her because I listened to her stories and believed what she was telling me. I trust way too easily and felt that she had no reason to mislead me. Because I believed everything she said, which was a lot, I believed that she was stronger, more powerful, more gifted than I was. In doing that – I gave her my power and opened myself up to being vulnerable. Based on what she said, I believed that she would never do anything considered 'dark'. That was the opening she needed and she took full advantage of it, to my detriment.

Drugs and alcohol

Without a doubt… and in every situation… drugs and alcohol attract undesirable energies.

When we are removed from our normal energy field, we open ourselves up to whatever "energy" that is available and intent on invading our space while we are unaware. "Drug beings" are discarnate humans who were addicted to drugs before making their transition and now they are stuck in the astral plane. These entities are always on the lookout to attach themselves to a living human so they can experience the physicality of doing the drugs again. "Alcohol beings" react in the same way. They're always looking for that next drink or binge, just like addicts in human form.

When we ingest mind altering substances, we weaken our auric field and chakra energy centers, making us defenseless against the invading negative energy. Our aura will tear or become full of holes and our chakras will either close down or open too widely, leaving us exposed to unpleasant energies that are difficult to manage. This is one of the reasons why people who become addicted to drugs or alcohol can appear 'clean', but can never shake the addiction. They're dealing with it from two levels… physically and thru an entity that's just (if not more) addicted than they are. Everyone I have ever met with an addiction has had at least one or two entities attached to them.

Mental Illness & Disability

Unfortunately in our society, we have those who suffer from mental illnesses and mental disabilities. Many were born into this situation because of their agreed-upon life plan and the lessons that that came hereto learn and experience. Others created this situation thru accidents, illness and sometimes physical abuse. None of these people are to be blamed for their conditions, neither are they to be pitied. They deliberately chose this path and from personal experience, I can tell you that there is so much more to them that what you see at first.

For the longest time, people believed that the mentally ill and disabled were possessed by demons. That's not necessarily true, as many of these people truly have beautiful souls and spirits. On occasion, I've run across very few mentally ill or disabled people who actually had negative entities attached to them, but this has been an extreme exception.

Granted, mental illness and mental disability leaves the person and their aura exposed and vulnerable, however, in working with the mentally disabled, I only found one person out of the 400 I regularly worked with to have a negative entity attached. Actually, I never noticed it… my horse did when we were doing animal therapy. This woman came up to him and he wanted nothing to do with her. Granted, this horse had been doing this type of therapy for over four years and had seen and put up with everything under the sun. He'd had wheelchairs run up under him, been poked in the eyes, ears, nose and mouth, had his tail pulled and one time had someone hanging on to his neck for dear life and screaming her head off in an effort to not have to leave the horse. He's stood firm and strong for hours, allowing people to touch and pet him, absorbing his loving and caring energy. But this one time, with this one woman, he wasn't having any of it and decided he needed to leave the area. He was great and perfectly behaved for two hours before the encounter and for another hour after that. He just knew and saw something that I didn't and decided that we needed to go to another area and group of people to visit. These animals… they know and see everything.

I have also had the opportunity to meet some amazingly gifted psychics and channels who were labeled mentally ill because family members and society didn't understand their gifts and what they were doing. These people were intelligent, personable and had a knowledge far superior to most of ours, but they would tell what they saw or channeled as a child and it frightened people, so they were sent away into institutions. Children have a much closer connection to their Angels and Guides, and will communicate with them while they're young. This is nothing to be alarmed about. In fact, in Chile it's the belief that for the first seven years of a child's life, they belong to the Angels and are encouraged to commune with them. What a beautiful upbringing that must be!

Just know that if you see or hear a child talk about their Angel friends in a loving way, that's really normal and not something that we should be afraid of . They don't need to see a psychotherapist or have an exorcism. Now if the Angels or imaginary friends are telling them something bad or dangerous, then it might be wise to have them questioned, by a professional, to ensure that they haven't picked-up an entity. This is extremely rare for children, the disabled and the mentally ill, so it shouldn't be a concern for anxious parents or grandparents. Your children are simply seeing their beloved friends from the other side.

I've also had the occasion to work with adults who have been diagnosed as being bi-polar. Most of them are very intuitive, which makes me wonder if they truly have the disease or if they are just "too open". I have dealt with them on good days, as well as bad ones, helping them to distinguish who they were listening to, their own mind, their Guides or a negative entity.

In the cases I've worked with, I've noticed that most of the people involved had an abnormally open crown chakra and they were receiving just a little too much energy. Once we performed chakra balancing and regulated the amount of energy that was flowing into them, they generally seemed to feel much better.

By no means is this meant to be a diagnosis, but simply an explanation of some of the experiences I've had with clients who heard voices and were diagnosed with a mental illness. I fully believe that we should embrace traditional medicine, along with alternative/complimentary medicine or energy work to complete the healing process for anything that occurs in the body or mind. I never want to rule-out potential medical issues. Once we know what's going on with the individual, then we attack the problem on an energetic level, to receive a complete and comprehensive resolution to the problem.

Physical Manifestations of a Psychic Attack

Below is a description of some of the most commonly reported physical symptoms that can arise as a result of a psychic attack.

Migraines: The veil between you and the outer realms could indeed be thin if you find yourself suffering from repeated migraines. Migraines are a kind of electromagnetic disorder that affects all of the major perception centers. Migraine symptoms include loss of vision, an altered sense of smell and increased sensitivity in hearing. In turn, these symptoms could be caused by an external attack from a toxic thought form sent to you and meant to poison your aura. Also, the shutting down of the senses associated with migraines could be described as one of the Seven Circles of Hell. Your body may be trying to deprive itself of its senses and force you to look inside your internal landscape to detect the source of the problem.

Occipital Headaches: These occur at the back of the neck. People who are under astral attack tend to be under a lot of stress. Many who visualize astral attack often picture the person being bludgeoned on the back of the head. Banging the victim's head against a wall is also a common fantasy.

Temporal Headaches: These are sharp pains that occur around the temples as a result of someone visualizing your head in some kind of vise. They may also be manipulating a doll with pins or nails to achieve the same effect.

Sinus Headaches: These can be the result of doll work, where the facsimile of you is being sprinkled or buried in some kind substance. Witches use everything from coffee grounds to kitty litter for these purposes. Sinus headaches can also be the result of emotional transfer, as sinus trouble typically represents unshed tears. If you have caused someone a lot of grief, they may be sending you their unshed tears— "now you feel what I feel."

Third Eye Headaches: This is more common in psychics and healers, and usually feels like a mild fuzzy pressure in the center of the forehead between the eyebrows. This can occur when one is trying to channel you with either a positive or negative message.

Jaw Pains: One of the most common statements made mentally about an absent individual is "I wish they would shut up." These feelings can be sent to you either consciously or unconsciously. Certain malicious rituals and spells also involve the binding of the jaw in order to silence an individual.

Visual Disturbances: Distortions of vision are usually caused by shifts in brain chemicals that force you to see wide angles or zigzags of light. On the astral level, this is commonly caused by a spirit invasion. This is something that a channeler or medium is more likely to experience than a non-practitioner.

Changes in Smell or Taste: An entity is usually responsible for this kind of symptom although someone playing with a voodoo doll can also trigger it. However if you are experiencing times when you suddenly smell something specific (i.e. cigarettes, strong perfume) that might be a sign that a spirit is trying to connect with you.

Stomach Cramps: Stomach cramps often symbolize an attack from either a group or an entity. The stomach or solar plexus is the center from which we connect to others. When a psychic enters a haunted area, often the first symptom that they experience is stomach cramps. This may also represent an attempt by a third party to disturb or tamper with your gut feelings. Stomach cramps can occur when an obsessed individual is trying to put a hook into your third chakra to connect you to them against your will.

Nausea: An upset stomach is associated with all forms of psychic aggression.

Diarrhea: People who are being overwhelmed by negative vibrations or soaking up too much astral information from others tend to suffer from this ailment. It is an emergency signal that the aura is trying to cleanse itself.

Hives: You may be having an allergic reaction to bad energy being sent to you. This may be the result of a doll or simulacrum-type magic where an offensive substance is covering a likeness of you.

Arthritis, Rheumatism or Restricted Movement: Both binding spells and freezer spells can cause an individual to become "paralyzed" and experience less mobility. A person may be trying to stop you from what you are doing or freeze you in your tracks.

Impotence or Lack of Sex Drive: A sudden inability to "get it up" is the aim of many spells that intend to separate you from a loved one. This is usually done using candles, binding, freezer magic and the manipulation of photographs.

Burning or Pins and Needles Feeling in the Extremities: Unfortunately, this may be caused exactly by what it sounds like. Someone may be visualizing or using a likeness of you as an actual pincushion.

Asthma: Many rituals and spells involve the visualization of the sucking of life energy or breath from an individual. Also the body may be naturally responding to what it perceives as an unseen threat.

If someone is imagining you drowning, you could suffer from asthma. There is also an entire set of rituals that involve smothering an individual by placing his or her image in a jar and corking it.

It is always important for you to have any physical symptoms checked out and treated by a medical doctor first. Although our belief is that many of these instances may involve negative energy, there are many times when it is necessary to receive traditional medical care.

Emotional Symptoms

Perhaps the most succinct way to describe the emotional effect of psychic attack is having emotions that you don't feel belong to you. For instance, you may spend all day feeling angry, when what is going on in your life does not support your anger. You may feel inexplicably sad, aroused, anxious, elated, happy or even maniacal. Most people who experience this sense whom the emotion is coming from and usually their first instinct is a big clue. This phenomena occurs mostly in codependent relationships, where two individuals are over-attached at the solar plexus or level of the third chakra.

Experiencing this kind of phenomena means you have a true psychic parasite on your hands. Almost always, this kind of attachment comes from someone who is living and has a history of upsetting your life. Alcoholics, manic-depressives and people with personality disorders are especially adept at this kind of astral invasion. Usually the object of the attack is an empathetic sort, and the invasion is not always intentional. Such forms of invasion are also common among parents and children.

Another effect of astral invasion or attack can be a loss of feeling towards those that you normally have feelings for. This could be the result of a binding spell, a freezer spell, or one of the thousands of Breaking-Up Spells that are out there in the public domain.

Generally, the loss of emotional control is thought to be a symptom of all forms of psychic invasion. It is a natural reaction to a disturbance in your aura. For instance, if you are in possession of an object that makes you feel great sadness, perhaps it is time to get rid of that object. If thinking about a specific individual makes you angry, stop thinking about that person.

More than 90% of the battle against psychic attack is detaching one's self from emotionally charged situations, bad memories and anticipation of a drama. On a psychic level, emotions tend to charge otherwise dormant situations or events. Also emotions lower your overall vibrations to their basest levels. According to the principle of "like attracts like," if you are demonstrating a lot of anger and grief you will probably attract situations and people who are similarly affected to you. Similar energy forms tend to aggregate in groups or clusters. The same is true of spirits. One way to resist this kind of effect is to not make yourself or your home a comfortable place for negative energy to take up permanent residence. Like most predators, if the spirit or thought form has nothing to feed off of, it will either starve to death or leave.

Psychological Disturbances

Anxiety is perhaps the most common psychological symptom associated with astral attack or invasion and is usually the result of a disturbed electromagnetic field.

Common types of anxiety that people experience while under astral attack are:

- The feeling that if they don't act on something right away that the world will end.
- An obsession with an object or a situation to the exclusion of all other thoughts.
- A sudden compulsion to go about one's daily affairs in a ritualistic or compulsive way.
- Attacks of panic or hysteria.
- Fear of the unknown, fear of known places or things, fear that one might not be able to handle what is to come in the immediate future, and fear that one might hurt others or oneself.

A ritual or violent thought form sent to you from other people can trigger these kinds of disorders. For instance, if someone has given you a car as a gift, and is uncertain about your ability to care for it, you might find yourself obsessed with the car. Or someone may be sending you a thought form in the shape of a monster or animal that you might be sensing as a threat. In certain Wiccan rituals, words are loaded with emotion and you might be picking up on the drama associated with that—these rituals are designed to cause anxiety.

Other kinds of visualizations and rituals act like Chinese water torture and are designed to slowly but surely beat down your defenses by creating consistently irritating situations. Also common are candle spells, where a spirit is summoned to give you no rest or no peace until you behave as desired by the magician.

Certain kinds of poppet magic can cause quirky effects in its targets including clumsiness, speech disorders, general disorientation, confusion and the desire to act out. For example, you might find yourself walking along the street, talking angrily to someone who isn't there. When an angry or jealous spirit possesses you, you might find yourself feeling those emotions more or displaying uncharacteristic behavior.

Those under the influence of a badly done love or lust ritual could suddenly become The humorous thing I have heard about love, lust and "come to me" spells is that usually the receiver of the ritual does not tend to become lusty towards the sender of the spell.
An inability to concentrate on anything could also indicate psychic interference from another person. The person who is upset with you and targeting you, whether they are using thought forms or ritual magic, is usually agitated at the time. It is quite easy for you to pick up on that agitation and be too flustered to go about your daily work.

Developing an unreasonable fear of water and avoiding baths or showers is also a symptom of psychic attack. Water is a conductor of psychic energy and your gut instincts are telling you that you are more vulnerable when you are wet. On the other hand – I often receive messages from my Angels and Guides much clearer when I'm in or around water, so this can be a positive thing, too.

Also common in cases of psychic attack or invasion is the feeling that there is a knot in your stomach or throat. Usually this effects the person's breathing and speech patterns. I often hear this in client's voices when they speak to me indicating that they have been blocked in the third (stomach) and fourth (throat) chakras. In this case usually the culprit is a living, mentally ill person who has astral hooks in the client and is enjoying a consistent feeding of emotional energy.

Feelings of depression, low self-esteem and fatigue can also be blamed on a psychic attack. This is usually due to a leak in your aura. Many people create a hole in their own aura in the hopes that it will allow an inaccessible individual in their life to reach them easier on the astral plane. It is important to make sure that it is not YOU who is attacking due to a neurotic need to substitute a real relationship with a spiritual one or a desire to draw someone closer to you.

Psychic vampires function by draining your energy which in turn causes irritation, fatigue and insomnia. Some people experience terrible feelings of restlessness and longing, or suffer from compulsive behaviors and thoughts. Often these symptoms are the result of an astral leeching, which visually can be described as hose with a sucker on the end embedded in your solar plexus. In this situation, you can become nothing more than a living battery for other individuals who have deemed it necessary to empower themselves by taking from you.

Sometimes a dream is just a dream, but there are certain structures to dream imagery that can indicate a psychic attack:

- ∞ Dreams that feature out-of-body experiences. This can be the result of an attack by a group mind who together, know how to lift your soul from your physical self and replace it, altered, back in your body.

- ∞ Dreams where you find yourself humiliated or confronted by groups or a round table of people. This is also indicative of a group attack.

- ∞ Dreams where you find yourself continually searching through malls and rooms for one person. This is one of those dreams that means the opposite. The person is with you, but your subconscious recognizes that the actual love in the relationship is missing.

- ∞ Dreams where someone is kissing you or trying to suck your breath. This is a typical invasive dream sent by someone who is suffering from unrequited love for you.

- ∞ Dreams that involve a great deal of water. Water symbolically represents psychic energy. Dreams that feature breaking dams or leaks may symbolize a leak caused by an attack on your aura.

- ∞ Dreams in which you are being threatened and chased by monsters or animals. In most schools of magic, mediums are taught to create thought forms or guardian animals that can invade the subconscious.

- ∞ Dreams involving weapons or appliance that directs a substance at your face. Many people use tools in their visualizations to direct bad energy at you.

- ∞ Dreams of being smothered, drowned, frozen or asphyxiated. There are many spells and rituals out there that contain this kind of component that could be picked up by your subconscious.

- ∞ Dreams where you are shown objects like notebooks, billboards or movies. Usually these artifices for storytelling represent a mechanism in magic where you are being sent a message.

- ∞ Dreams where you are telephoned, but you pick up the phone and nobody is there. Usually, in a healthy dream, you receive a message. The lack of voice on the other line represents the secrecy around most rituals.

The purpose of a psychic attack is to destroy the container of the personality so that it eventually cracks. In severe cases, astral attack can cause compulsive, morbid thoughts, disassociation from reality and hallucinations.

Spiritual Symptoms

Believe it or not, an increased interest in spiritual things, the New Age Movement, religion and the occult can represent a psyche that is suffering from astral or psychic attack.

When you are being drained by a psychic attack you may feel the need or compulsion to heal yourself or supplement your energy by seeking a healer, channeler, guru or religious group. The very idea that you need this extra support may imply that your spiritual vessel is somehow leaking or been emptied.

Although such support can be helpful, it can, ironically, also betray a deep lack of faith, not only in oneself but also in the goodness of whatever power is up there. Ironically, most people who are seeking spiritual guidance are actually fighting what they believe God or a Higher Power has in store for with them. It is a form of resistance to being on the "right" spiritual path.

One important symptom of psychic attack is the inability to distinguish between good and evil. Long-term victims of repeated psychic attacks often suffer a kind of moral malaise. They also frequently express a lack of faith in a Higher Power and in goodness. They will insist this is the product of logic, when this kind of existentialism is the result of spiritual fatigue because of third-party interference.

The intent of most psychic attacks is to separate us from our will and our faith. It leads us to put our trust in gurus and false prophets. Even if the guru or prophet is genuine, we cause damage to ourselves by failing to recognize that the vessel for the spirit is separate from the vessel itself.

Another spiritually related symptom of psychic invasion is an increased attention to what I would call omens or signs. Sometimes this phenomenon is just a stage of the grieving process. A typical scenario is a woman left by her lover for another, who keeps thinking that she is receiving astral messages from him in the form of coincidences—the constant playing of a favorite song, seeing people who resemble him or have his name and other synchronistic encounters. This psychological glitch keeps the griever in denial of what really happened because she is not emotionally ready to accept the reality of it. On the other hand, a persistence of this kind of coincidence can mean a psychic attack, especially if the messages seem malevolent. Often too, when a person deliberately weakens his aura in the hopes that it will bring him nearer to a lost dear one, other entities and thought forms attach themselves to the person, compelling him to more obsessive behavior. The absent person becomes like God—if the color blue was God, you would see blue everywhere. The same is for the object of obsession. You have let this person become your God.

Healthy individuals with healthy auras are not superstitious. They vibrate at a level of faith that is so high, not even witchcraft can harm them.

Situational Symptoms

If you experience any of the following situational symptoms you may be under psychic attack:

Constantly Losing Objects: This could be the result of someone wishing loss on you on a consistent basis or you may be the victim of a ritual that was designed to disorient and confuse you.

Always Missing the Goal: People under psychic attack usually find themselves working hard, yet constantly confronting obstacle after obstacle. Success is often right within reach and then snatched from grasp. This frustration is also a punishment built into many rituals and spells.

Loss of Prosperity, Health and Family. Many spells are done exactly to achieve that intention.

Monkey on Your Back: Victims of curses may find themselves confronting a long-term difficult problem—such as an ongoing court case or unsolvable health or financial problem.

Friendships and Relationships Ending Abruptly for No Reason: People come into your life and then leave with no explanation. This is a form of evil-eye transference. Sometimes a ritual has been performed to cause others to find you repulsive. In other cases it is the result of an implant or energy transference to your aura that other people's instincts interpret as "negative energy." However, it is not really your energy. It is an astral implant that has been sent to you from somewhere else.

Mirroring: This is an effect that causes others to immediately mirror your actions back to you in an unpleasant fashion. For instance if you comment on a person being overweight, five minutes later, someone comments on your weight. Some rituals are designed to accelerate your Karma and create psychic pressure to make you feel lonely or like you need to get help from the attacker.

Attracting Accidents and Violent Situations: A repeated series of accidents or violence can be evidence of a ritual done by an individual that is wishing you harm. Auras that have been weakened by consistent psychic attack also tend to invite a multiple number of psychic attacks from other sources. As I have mentioned before, there are many people doing witchcraft who are not trained in the art. As a result, their misfires hit innocent people. A person walking around with a weak, leaky or damaged aura becomes a sitting duck for these stray energies on the astral plane.

Environmental Symptoms

Some places just have "bad vibes." Most people can detect these bad vibes and use words to describe them like "heavy," "tiring," "dead", "exhausting," or "draining." Sometimes this is because the place is actually inhabited by entities or spirits that feed off of human energy fields. Other times it is the result of an astral imprint left by an extremely dramatic and negative situation that took place there, such as a murder or a rape. These kind of energies are also felt on the sites of old graveyards and places where wars have been fought and bodies left unburied after slaughter.

In natural locations, these vibes can be attributed to the lingering spirit of a ritual done by a group. In terms of Feng Shui, the ancient art of Chinese Object Placement, astral stress can be caused by the following factors:

• A front door facing a road with oncoming traffic.
• A front door facing a church, graveyard or other place of religious worship.
• A view that is dwarfed by a large building.

All of these factors prevent the easy flow of life energy through your home and affect the aura adversely. There is a huge relationship between the health of the aura and the art of Feng Shui. If you feel that you are under psychic attack, the use of fountains, mirrors, trees, fences and wind chimes can substantially lower your odds of suffering geopathic stress in urban areas. Bad energy likes to conglomerate in the dark alleys of our urban areas just as much as criminals do.

The following are the most common environmental symptoms of psychic attack:

Constant Dysfunction: Chaos reigns. No matter how much you try to maintain order, the place constantly slides into a state of decay. Appliances, plumbing and other matters have to constantly be serviced or maintained. This could be the result of spirits playing tricks on you or the result of a ritual attack that has ordered the disintegration of your affairs.

Weird Odors and Smells: This can be an indication that your house is possessed by a foul spirit that was already there or that a spirit has been sent to you by a practitioner. It is also a sign of a weakened aura.

Problems with Electricity or Batteries: Some spirits and entities seem to feed off of electrical energy. Flickering lights, electrical shocks, appliances that turn on by themselves and batteries that die before their time are all symptoms of psychic attack.

Stopped Time Pieces: Spirits from other realms exist on a plane where there is no time. In some haunted houses, it is almost impossible to run a clock that keeps correct time.

Unusual Light: Some spirits or astral imprints represent themselves by a glow or an astral shaft or light that appears out of nowhere.

Poltergeist Activity: Objects that move by themselves, mysterious bumping and moaning in the night and everything else you've seen in horror movies falls into this category. These could be the spirits of former residents that have been sent to you via a ritual. Poltergeist activity can also be blamed on an aura that has been weakened by trauma, negativity, envy and resentment. Poltergeists like to feed on negative energy emitting from humans. Therefore, if you suffer from jealousy, you are likely to attract a jealous spirit. Psychics or healers that have become overstressed from work may also be releasing negativity that manifests in the form of poltergeist activity.

4

What is psychic protection?

Psychic protection is subtle and invisible, and it works on a non-physical level of being, to protect the body. It surrounds us with a protective barrier where we can safely expand our spiritual perception and go about our daily life. It works on an invisible, vibrational level and can be enhanced by utilizing the additional vibrational energy fields of crystals, visualizations, and flower essences.

Ultimately, psychic protection is about being fully grounded in your body. If you're not grounded, you'll never feel fully secure.

Thanks to the recent explosion of consciousness and the internet, information that normally was revealed to those who were ready for it, is now available to everyone. The internet can provide you with banishing spells, curses, rituals… you name it! You can learn these techniques yourself or now you can order a spell to be cast on your behalf online. With the proliferation of these websites and people getting into things that they're not ready for or don't understand, we've got a lot of negative stuff going on in the world.

By reading a couple of websites, some people will then start to cast spells against someone they perceive has done them wrong, not understanding the implications or severity of what they are doing. For those of us who are empaths, this type of reckless energy meddling can be almost crippling.

We have people blowing-open chakras, without understanding that it's not what should be done, they're opening portals to places where they have no business – then not closing them back. They go into dark realms exploring, then bring negative entities back with them… it's just gotten crazy in this world!

We've also been inundated with books and manuals about being a Light Worker, so someone can buy one of these books and proclaim themselves to be a 'Master', without actually doing anything. There are online PhD's in every subject for about $75, so everyone can be an expert.

These people do the opposite – they hang their shingle out as healers, shamans and teachers, when they don't have the first clue about what they're really doing. This, too, can be dangerous because if they see or try to help someone who has a problem with a negative entity… they can actually make it worse.

If you suffer from any of the symptoms listed previously, you're not protecting yourself enough and are most likely being psychically attacked. Protecting yourself is easy to do… and easy to forget about, until it's too late. We need to remember to cleanse and clear ourselves several times a day, depending on what's going on in our lives and where we're going.

We also need to be aware that we can inadvertently psychically attack someone else. If we have a disagreement with someone and just can't let it go… wishing harm to that person (things we've all said and done), our thoughts reach that person. As we all know, thoughts have energy and that energy will affect the person they're directed to.

Keep in mind Dr. Emoto's experiments with water… negative thoughts and words WILL and DO have an effect on living things. Unconsciously we are not only sabotaging the other person, but ourselves. We're right back to that old Karma thing again!

Psychic protection needs to be something simple, that you can do in a second to protect yourself, but can also be something that you have in place to keep you, your family and your home safe and secure. If you come up with some type of complicated or detailed ritual for your daily protection, the majority of us will only do it 1-2 times a month and forget about it the rest of the time, leaving us wide-open.

We're going to talk about a lot of different methods of protection – for yourself, the family, home, work, traveling. Some are centuries old, some are brand new. Some are detailed, while others are surprisingly simple and obvious. What's the best method? Whatever feels the most comfortable to you and that you'll do!

Our first level of defense is our aura. These subtle energies expand out from us, interacting with everything around us. This is how empaths pick-up on the thoughts, feelings and emotions of other people. It's also how those who are desperate for energy act as vampires, stealing-away energy of others. If our aura is strong, then we'll be well-protected, but if it's been damaged by trauma, illness, or shock, it can have "breaks", "tears" or a weakness. Geopathic stress and electromagnetic radiation can also weaken our auras, making us more vulnerable to negative influences and psychic invasion.

Some psychics are gifted and able to "see" the aura, including all the emotions and attachments within it. They can let us know if our aura is healthy and strong, or if there are problems with it. However most of us are unable to "see" them. But, as long as you are aware of your aura and focus on strengthening its ability to protect you, you'll be able to safeguard yourself against unwanted intrusions or energy leakage.

5

Visualizations for Protection

This is an excellent way to begin protecting yourself psychically. Take a few minutes, twice a day, (just to get started) for this visualization in order to increase the amount of protection that your aura is able to provide. Even if you're unable to visualize clearly, try this exercise to increase your protective abilities.

The Light Bubble

Take a few minutes to relax and close your eyes. Breathe out any tension you may be feeling – while breathing in a sense of peace and relaxation. Take as long as you need to gradually withdraw your attention from the outside world and into yourself.

Look up to your inner screen and project a picture of a place where you feel happy and protected. It may be a grassy glade, a beach, a church, a garden, a place from your childhood. This can be an actual place or one from your imagination. Think about this place and it will appear on your screen. Spend a few minutes enjoying that place, remembering how good it feels to be there. Let your senses bring you the smell of this place, its own unique, fragrant perfume. Let your skin show you the warmth of this place. Is there a breeze softly blowing or raindrops from a summer shower?

While you are enjoying your special place, know that this is your sacred room – you can come back here at any time to visit, to re-energize yourself, to rest and re-charge. You are always safe here!

As you are standing here in your sacred space, picture a copper cord running from the bottom of your feet, deep down into the earth. This cord holds you in this incarnation. It is flexible, allowing you to move, but is hooked into the core of the earth, anchoring your physical body in everyday reality. With this cord in place, you will always be grounded and centered.

Gradually you'll become aware that there is a shaft of bright Light shining down and touching the ground in front of you. This Light pulsates with energy and flashes of color. It can be a special color that you need at this time, or it may be white, containing all the colors of the rainbow.

Allow yourself to step into this Light. Stand within it and absorb the light into your whole being. Breathe it in, absorb it through your skin and allow it to permeate your aura. Fill your aura with Light and vitality. After a while, you will become conscious of your aura stretching out around you in vibrant color. See the different colored layers flowing out from and around your body. Check your aura's level of vitality; if you need more, breathe in more Light. If it is too powerful, let it settle and find its appropriate level.

Notice how far out your aura extends. Feel its edges. You can use your physical hands to reach out all around you, probing its limits. You will find that it is roughly egg-shaped, extending over your head, down to below your feet. Check and feel if it has any breaks or weaknesses. Experiment with your aura: pull it in close to you, allow it to widen out again. Let it settle, ending at an appropriate distance from your physical body. Knowing the boundary of your aura protects you, so spend as long as you need to become familiar with it.

If you feel you need extra protection, you can "crystallize" your aura's outer edge, making it strong and hard, but translucent so you can see out. You will be encased in an egg-shaped crystal full of Light.

When you are ready, step out from the column of Light. Check that your aura is still glowing, full of this beautiful, Divine Light. Check that its boundary is strong and intact. It should be completely surrounding you, forming an impenetrable protective barrier around you. This is your cloak of protection. Nothing can cross your aura unless you choose to allow it. Nothing can drain its energy and vitality. You are protected. When you are wearing this cloak, this radiant protective aura, nothing can intrude or impress itself on you. You can wrap the cloak around yourself, reaching from the top of your head to the bottom of your feet, and it will give you complete protection. You can open your cloak if you want your psychic energies to interact with someone else. Once you've finished your interaction or meditation, ensure that the cloak is wrapped firmly around yourself. This is your protection — your bubble of Divine Light. Know that you are completely protected, safe and secure while you are in this Light.

When you are ready, gently bring your awareness back into the room. Be aware of your physical body, of your feet on the earth. Breathe a little more deeply. Move your hands and feet. Get up and stretch. Be aware of your aura and its protective function. From now on, you will live within a bubble of Divine Light protecting you from harm.

Even if you are non-visual, you can still feel the energy of your aura and its outer edges. They may feel spongy, tingly, warm… you'll know it when you discover this. Once you know how far your aura stretches, sense the white Light surrounding it, feel its warmth and brightness.

6

The Power of Thought

Thought is the most powerful force on this planet. It is the impulse that sets things in motion, that creates, and that destroys. Thought is an extremely powerful tool in our psychic armory. What we believe in, we bring into being. To believe in ourselves is our strongest protection. If we know, at the deepest level of our being, that nothing can touch us, then we have perfect protection.

Once we acknowledge that thoughts are actual things, and that we're all connected, we'll cease to inflict harm both on ourselves and others.

We've all had the experience of having a thought pop into our head that wasn't exactly ours. We've picked it up telepathically from somewhere, because we KNOW it wasn't our thought. These thoughts come to us on the psychic level. Some people are bombarded with these thoughts, while others rarely have it happen. I have a client who experiences this several times a day and we have been working steadily to stop the flow of messages to her. How often it happens to someone depends on how open their aura is and how much they choose to allow this to happen. If your aura is open or has weak spots, then you'll be more vulnerable to psychic attack. If this is happening to you, spend some time with the Light Bubble meditation to get that protective cloak around you again, shielding you from anything that you don't need.

The power of thought has been used by cultures since time began. This is where curses come from. It's the belief in the curse that actually causes the problem… not necessarily the curse itself, although curses do have powers and can affect us. This has happened with native cultures for thousands of years. The local witch-doctor would curse someone and they would immediately fall ill. It was really the victim's belief system that made them ill, because once they believed that they were cursed their body had no choice but comply with the thought patterns.

The victim will take the information in, believe it and manifest the consequences. However, it's difficult to prove to curse victims that the curses aren't valid, because they'll always have just a little bit of doubt, thinking: "What if it's real?" That little thought always leaves the door open to something manifesting with the doubt.

The thought or fear of a curse is enough to by-pass most all belief systems. Most people are still going to wonder if it's real... if it's true. This is how all those witch-doctors, priests, shamans, witches and others were able to have power over indigenous peoples so many years ago. The people were terrified of the curse (and the performance accompanying it), so naturally they manifested the consequences.

Once the victim has allowed the process of fear and doubt in, then it allows their own negative beliefs to go into overdrive. We program ourselves to believe that something horrible is going to happen to us, no matter how irrational that thought process is. This undermines anything positive that we're doing and brings about the dire outcome. Remember that *we manifest what we believe*. This also sets us up to create a negative energy grid, attracting negative energies which will also speed-up the process of something negative happening.

Another way that our thought processes betray us is by believing that "He/she is more powerful than I am." This lays us open to psychic dominance and can also make us suffer consequences. If you believe that someone else is more powerful than you are, then you're just asking to have your own abilities downplayed. Besides... none of us are on the same path and we don't all have the same gifts. You simply can't compare yourself or another person to someone else.

The same thing goes with prosperity… if we say "You poor thing, you're never going to get a job," guess what? He'll never get a job because we're helping program his thought processes to prevent him from going out and getting a great job. People do this to each other and themselves all the time, in every facet of life, even when they don't mean any harm.

Saying and believing these things makes us feel powerless, helpless and at the mercy of outside forces. If you believe, with all your heart, that you are all-powerful and in control of your life, then situations can and will change for you overnight. This is how people become great at manifesting… they BELIEVE in themselves. They know they can do it!

Once we learn to focus our thoughts and to program them to be positive, rather than negative, we'll create the best protection that we can possibly have. This is the power and strength behind creative visualization. It's not the actual images that are powerful, but the concentrated thought we put into creating the thoughts that brings the results. The images are simply a focus for our intention. This is one of the reasons why "acting as if" is so important when you have difficulty visualizing. Don't let this stop you! If you allow yourself to feel the process, listen to your inner voice, act as if you are seeing, and most importantly have the intention, then the Universe will act on your belief and make things happen.

For those who choose to attack, the reverse is true. They focus their resentment, rage, anger, bitterness and hatred into a concentrated ball of thought – then hurtle it towards their victim through the psychic airwaves. If the intended "victim" doesn't have protection, this 'ball of hatred' will slam into their thoughts and minds with tremendous force. If the "victim" has strong protection, it can be transmuted into love and blessings for that intended "victim". How is that possible? When you are doing your visualization meditation, simply ask that anything negative that is sent your way be transmuted into love, light, abundance and blessings for you. That's a wonderful way to fend-off negative energies or attacks because it amplifies the level of good things that come into your life!

Keep in mind that when you're in a situation where you feel that you need to boost or increase your psychic protection, always remind yourself that, "I can do this. I have the power to face anything that comes my way." If this is difficult for you to say, practice standing in front of a mirror a couple times each day, telling yourself the following:

"I am a beautiful child of God. I have amazing gifts and am powerful in many ways.
I can   face anything that comes my way and
I **overcome any and all adversity**.
There is no stopping me on my path for love and light."

You can say something along these lines. Whatever phrases you feel most comfortable with are just fine. Remember that it's vitally important for you to have confidence in your ability to protect yourself… but not so much that you turn into a bully. Don't ever forget our friend, Karma, because she'll always remember you!

Thanks to physics, we know that "like attracts like", so if you claim to be powerful and have loving, positive thoughts… that's what you'll attract into your life. If you keep your vibrations high, through prayer, meditation, working with crystals, healing, music, etc. then you'll attract people who are the same way. If you keep your intentions for the highest and greatest good for all (without being egotistical or making it 'all about you'), then you will achieve that good. If your thoughts are pure, then you will manifest good. If you raise your vibrations to their highest level, then you can reach your Higher Self - that part of you that is at the highest vibration.

Beating Negative Thoughts

We've talked about the power of positive thoughts and now it's time to focus on the more negative ones. If someone decides to send that 'ball of hatred' to you, how can you deal with it? There are several ways you can protect yourself:

~ First and foremost, wrap yourself in your cloak if protection. Do your visualization each morning before you get your day started. You can always do a "tune-up" later in the day or if you feel like you need a little boost.

~ Work with any of the protection methods we have listed to create a shield around you, your home and your family.

~ If there is a particular person who is sending you these negative energies, visualize putting a net or a wet dishtowel over them to stop their attack. Imagine how ineffective someone would be with a giant dripping-wet dishtowel draping over their head and shoulders.

~ Stock up on Black Tourmaline or obsidian. These are excellent stones to filter and transmute negative energy. They block attacks and clear the air. Wear them, keep some in your house and in your office. Place them near the computer and telephone to filter and clear negativity that comes across the airwaves. These stones have been used as protection for thousands of years and they work great.

~ Visualize the attacks that the person is sending your way and wrap them inside a giant bubble. This bubble can be any color – whatever you prefer is fine. Once they are finished filling the bubble with their anger, allow it to float away. As this bubble floats high in the sky, imagine it bursting, releasing harmless little droplets spreading over a wide area and doing harm to no one.

~ You can visualize a giant mirror that is moving close to the person wishing you harm… reflecting all their nastiness right back to them. Or place them in a mirror box, close and lock the lid. Now they're trapped inside with mirrors reflecting their negativity in a hundred different ways!

~ Permanently cut your cords with that person. If someone is affecting you this strongly, it means that there are psychic cords attaching the two of you. If you can't cut the cords yourself (visualize it being like an electrical plug & just un-plug them from your body), have an energy-worker do this for you. It's easy and can make a difference very quickly.

~ If the attack is coming from someone who isn't very strong and you are aware of it, you can visualize that person surrounded with a pink glow and light of love and forgiveness. This pulls the rug right out from under them and strips them of their power. I like to add this technique to some of the other ones, as a way to finish my protection.

Sometimes we can become the victim of a psychic attack, that's from a spirit or entity. First of all, we need to assess whether the entity just 'appeared' or if we actually called them to us. If you're playing with Ouija boards, opening portals, doing séances, channeling or calling-in the dead for entertainment purposes, then you're doing yourself and those spirits a huge disservice. If this happens, you generally will need the assistance of an experienced Lightworker to help guide this entity back to where it needs to be… not just banishing it from your immediate area.

This can generally be performed using space-clearing techniques, working with the Highest Spiritual Guidance, as well as incense, sage, crystals, holy water and/or essences and can often take a while to accomplish. When this occurs, it's almost like performing an exorcism on the home and people; and it puts people at risk. Just *don't invite these entities into your home and everything and everyone will be much safer for it.*

7

Personal Psychic Shields

There are many ways to create a psychic shield and I haven't heard of any that I would consider to be 'wrong'. The most important thing is that you do one, some or all of these things each and every day to ensure that you are safe energetically. The only thing that I would consider to be 'wrong' is if you were to wrap yourself in dark or black light instead of the colors or white. Otherwise experiment with these techniques to fine one you're comfortable with.

Shield of Light

Close your eyes and circle an imaginary ring of pure, white light about six inches over the head, then quarter with a cross (there are other symbols that will work just as well but for most western mediums the cross has most meaning and protective ability). From this cross in a circle of light draw down over the head and body a protective sheath of shining white light that ends under the feet. This should then be joined under the feet.

Orb of Light

This can easily be combined with the method above. Image an orb of white (or blue if this seems more effective) light hovering and sending out rays of light about 9 inches to a foot above the crown of the head. Some people link this to the head or third eye with a strand of light but I have not found this to be necessary.

Colors in Protection

Everyone likes to add a little color in their life. When you give your energy its own color, you are personalizing it and making it easier for you to relate to. Some people are very firm in the belief that white energy is the purest and therefore is most powerful. Generally white and blue are the most commonly used colors for psychic protection. There may be something to this, but it is always best to listen to your gut. If you feel an urge to have a green shield, then go with it. You can always experiment by changing your shield's color every week. If you find one shade or tone to be more effective than others, then stick with it.

You can shield yourself with specific colors, depending on your intention. Know that your intention to surround yourself with this light won't be denied – anyone who asks will receive, without exception. The following colors will help you in very specific ways:

- ∞ **White Light** – This invokes the Angels around you to surround you without interruption. The Angels protect you, and they ensure that you're safe and guarded.

- ∞ **Pink Light** – This is the light to invoke if you're with a negative person who's obsessed with their problems. The pink light sends loving energy outward toward everyone who talks with you, and simultaneously sends loving energy inward toward yourself. Nothing can permeate this pink shield except loving thoughts and energies.

- ∞ **Emerald Green Light** – See or feel yourself surrounded by this light whenever you want to heal some imbalance in your physical body. Your body absorbs this light whenever it needs healing energy.

- ∞ **Purple Light** – Imagine yourself shrouded in royal purple light, which elevates your spiritual frequency, enabling you to rise above problems and contact the highest level of Divine guidance. Purple light also bounces away any lower energies, entities, or earthbound spirits.

- ∞ **Rainbow Light** – See or feel yourself wearing a coat of rainbow stripes, which boosts your ability to conduct energy healing work on yourself or others.

You can shield yourself in layers of multi-colored light if you choose, in order to invoke all of the beneficial effects of the various colors.

Complex combinations of color can be used to create very strong protection. For example you could make a shield that starts as red at the top of your head and then slowly graduates to orange, yellow, green, blue and then purple when it finally reached your feet. Visualizing such a shield takes strong focus, and holding it this image in your mind's eye as the day goes by can be challenging. Since the appearance of this shield requires much more effort, it is more strongly empowered by your will. Unusual patterns in shields can also aid you in psychic self-defense. Integrating a religious design or an occult symbol that represents protection can add extra strength and power.

Pulsating Light Defense

This is a very strong defense and personally I have only used it at times of great worry. Imagine the whole body as a dynamo able to produce pulses of intense white (or blue) light. Then image these pulses being transmitted into the ether. Concentrate on these pulses and send them out rapidly and strongly. Always re-enforce with the shield of light and later the orb of light.

The Golden Cross

I have found this effective as a way of distinguishing "good" and "deceptive/bad" spirits. I am not sure if it is the symbolism that works or whether it serves as a way to concentrate and better distinguish their nature. As you sense the spirit form concerned, mentally hang a golden cross (other potent symbols may serve just as well) with a golden chain round its neck. Spirits that you do not want are unable to stand this and will often flee. Better spirits will seem enhanced.

Sealing oneself

If you feel threatened in any way, bring your energies back into the center of your body by concentrating your attention there. At the same time, quiet your thoughts as far as you can. You can also, if you wish, visualize yourself surrounded by a tube of light, a transparent cylinder tough as steel which extends above your head and beneath your feet. Your Higher Self can release it to you at your request. But with visualizations, you have to relate to them and work with them in quiet times before you need them.

Mummy Technique

The visualizing of specific shapes forming around your body piece by piece adds focus and resolve to your psychic protection, and this is the basis of the mummy technique. Begin by creating the image of a ball of white light glowing just above your head where the crown chakra or higher-self psychic center is located. Focus on the energy here, willing its intensity to increase. Visualize white light sweeping down from this powerful sphere in the shape of a wide ribbon that begins to wrap around your head. You may want to leave some space between the energy ribbons and your physical body, perhaps 3-4 inches. Have the ribbon continue to wrap around your head, overlapping itself and creating a solid sheet that surrounds your head in protective energy. Don't stop at the head though. Let the ribbon continue to spin around your shoulders, torso, hips, legs - all the way down to the feet, making sure to cover every spot so that you are entirely and safely wrapped. Once you've worked your way down to your feet, have it wrap underneath them, completing the blanket surrounding you. When you are completely wrapped, hold the image of what you just did in your mind for a few moments before opening your eyes. This exercise is a great way to improve your skills with energy manipulation while benefiting yourself.

Burning Flame

The Burning Flame is best used in situations that may be dangerous or that you require a great amount of psychic protection over a short period of time. If you are entering a place/meeting/situation with a terrible amount of negativity you can perform this technique. Some people visualize their shields as a fire surrounding them at all times which is fine, although the method presented here is geared toward an emergency situation or on a temporary basis since it uses high amounts of energy. The Violet Flame is extremely effective in these situations, but other colors can be used, as well.

Stand perfectly upright with your legs together and your arms flat against your side. Go deep inside yourself to the center of your being. Approach all of this with a confident intensity, your mind focused on your need for protection. Find your center and know that in your center is an intense source of energy, the very energy that all your magical abilities come from. With your consciousness in this core of your being, create an eruption of energy within yourself. Like a volcano building up pressure, cause your energy to rise and expand from your center out. As the energy reaches the outside of your body have it burst into a blue flame that surrounds your body. The curved base of the flame should be at your feet and the tip of the flame above your head. The intense energy flame will burn any outside vibrations before they can reach you. This flame won't harm you physically since it's a spiritual flame, but it will stop any other spirit or energy from touching you. Once the flames surround you, try to keep part of your mind focused on it as you proceed through the situation you felt required extra psychic protection. Imagine more energy fanning the flames stronger and higher as you exhale.

As with any of these techniques, practicing first in a safe place is highly recommended.

Chakra Spin Protection

This powerful technique unites the chakras to create a shield fully embedded with all aspect of your will and energy. Visualize yourself charging the crown chakra, and draw a line down to the 3rd eye chakra. Charge the 3rd eye before drawing a line to the throat. Charge and continue to the heart, charge this chakra and draw a line of white light to the solar plexus chakra. After charging the solar plexus you move to the sacral chakra, charge it and then onto the root chakra. This is an adaptation of the traditional chakra system to have a center between the two feet so draw one more line to the ground center and charge this area. Create two lines of light from this center that swoop to each side of you in an upward curve before connecting with the crown chakra above your head. Begin cycling your energy through the lines timed with your breathing.

Instead of stopping at this point, continue cycling but move your focus to the curved lines at your side. We want to move these two lines simultaneously clockwise so that they being to spin around the body. Let them put out energy as they continue to move faster and faster until their light forms a solid wall of energy that surrounds you. Spin this wall of energy around you for a few moments. When you feel ready, let the image of the chakras fade from your mind, and let the spinning motion end, but hold onto the image of all the energy the chakras surrounded you with.

Mirror Shield

Another way to shield is after you have visualized being encapsulated in the White Light envision a circle of mirrors around that facing outward. Do not visualize these mirrors reflecting the negativity BACK to whomever it came from but rather upwards towards the heavens to be dissipated. Intend that this mirror will stand between you and your attacker as long as necessary. This will help stop the influx of energy coming in your direction. It will also be of less karmic impact than the other mirror methods.

Marshmallow/Sticky Shield

The Marshmallow Shield is a thick, sticky type of shield. Its primary purpose is to absorb attacks and hold them for later disposal. It can be programmed to dissolve the simple attack or just spit it back out. When you are visualizing this shield, you want to picture a thick wall of goo, if you construct it in layers you will want to make sure the layers melt into each other completely.

This shield can take a while to make, but it is not meant to be used as the only line of defense. Combine it with other defensive shields to provide better protection.

The Blanket Technique - Protecting Others Psychically

As you become more comfortable and skilled in protecting yourself, there will be times when you may want to shield another person or loved one. You can extend the protection skills you have honed for yourself to help others as long as it is their free choice and will to accept your protection.

Visualize a dot of pure blue light, increase this light's intensity until it burns very bright. Take this dot and trace out a square twice as big as the person you are going to shield. When you trace the outline of the blanket, its lines should stay visible in your mind's eye. Once the outline is complete, begin to pour universal protective energy into the square shape. While you are filling the square with energy, be sure to program the protective powers you want to be inherent within. Think of the specific circumstance that they are seeking protection from and instill this energy with the power to resist and repel it. Hold this image in your mind's eye for a good minute before letting it go. Keep in mind without being connected to any replenishing energy source, this shield is not going to last as long unless you program a period for the energy to last.

The Cosmic Cross of White Fire

Once you have practiced visualizing light you can use the thought form of the cross as it exists on the inner planes: the vertical bar symbolizing Spirit descending into matter and the horizontal bar signifying the matter plane. It is a giant cross ablaze with white fire, and you can visualize it standing in any terrible situation such as we see nightly on the news.

To work with it you can extend your arm full length and draw the cross with two extended forefingers of your right hand while saying aloud: "In the Name of the Christ (or in the Name I AM THAT I AM) I invoke the Cosmic Cross of White Fire upon…" whatever it is you wish the cross to counteract.

You may be troubled with a horrible memory or thought projection or even an image from a film which will not go away. Sometimes an evil picture can be pushed right up against the victim's face and it seems impossible to push it back. Children are especially vulnerable and can be taught to use the Cosmic Cross of White Fire to completely cover the image and burn it up. Even if the unwanted image does not completely disappear it can be neutralized so that it loses its power.

Thought forms such as this should always be invoked in the Name of I AM or of the Christ, and if in doubt as to whether you should use them you can ask for them to be adjusted according to Divine Will.

The Great Sun Disc

Even easier to visualize than the Cosmic Cross is this blazing, white-fire sun which symbolizes God and was once worshipped as such. It has immense power. You can visualize a huge, incandescent sun placed over your solar plexus as a shield against unwanted influences or emotional disturbance. In fact, the possibilities of visualization are unlimited, since we are dealing directly here with the Divine Light. I have frequently used this sun image in illness and physical injury.

As always, the more you practice and build up a relationship with these thought forms the more powerful they become. You have to treat them with reverence and love if you really want to benefit from them. They are of course perfectly real and intelligent.

Cutting The Cord

This classic ritual is a good way to sever yourself from a psychic vampire or entity that you may feel is leeching energy from you.

Sometimes, after a relationship has ended, many of us have problems letting go. Many of my clients complain of feeling haunted or even possessed by a dearly departed (who probably isn't even thinking of you and is busy with his or her new partner). It's like the person has left an indelible imprint upon your heart and you feel you can't go on unless that person or relationship returns. The energy of this person might be manifesting itself in all sorts of ways—in what you perceive as omens or reminders that occur in everyday life (such as a phrase or song lyric) or even as a visitor in your dreams.

There are all kinds of cures for this phenomenon (everything from burning bundles of sage to clear the room of the ex's vibe to throwing out every single reminder of him or her, including the bed). Yet before you do anything drastic, I suggest you try this little exercise called "Cutting the Cord."

The idea behind this is that whenever we connect to someone we connect to him or her at the point of our solar plexus, the area just below your diaphragm. When we first meet someone and fall in love, we spend a lot of time building up this energy which Light Workers say looks like a rope of light connecting two people.

However, even after one person disappears, the rope can still remain. Often, the person who is left behind spends a lot of time fortifying that rope with his or her own psychic energy in an attempt to bring the person back. The ex can be compared to a psychic vampire gleefully sucking back the energy that the dumped person is sending out. It doesn't matter if you are sending bad thoughts or resentment to him or her, that energy is often translated in the purest form of psychic energy, and used to transmute and feed the new relationship. Thus, in order to prevent yourself being sucked dry by the psychic vampire, I suggest you try this:

Lie down on the bed, breathe deeply and become as relaxed as you can. Now picture the other person and the cord of light that you created when you thought the both of you would be connected for all eternity. Visualize that cord as best you can and examine it. How thick is it? What color is it? What is it made of? Now choose your weapon. What will you use to cut this cord? Do you need a knife or is the connection so strong that it can be broken only by hacking at it with a machete? If a machete doesn't work, try a buzz saw. My favorite weapon is a huge pair of golden scissors. Now, in your mind's eye, snip, hack, chop, sever...do whatever you have to do to cut the cord.

Picture the other person floating away from you like a helium balloon let loose in the sky...and smile and wave "bye-bye!" Oddly, one of the side benefits to this ritual is that the other person senses the detachment. Like a villain returning to the scene of the crime, the vampire will return to see where their source of energy has gone. So not only does this exercise your psychic health, but it often brings the other person back. That is, if you want them back at all.

The Love Meditation

Believe it or not, you don't always have to fight fire with fire. You can put out a fire with water. The psychic equivalent of water is love. It involves visualizing the attacker. If you don't know who it is, you can still ask for loving energy to be sent to the right target.

This meditation is good for almost all forms of psychic attack that you feel originates from a person—living or dead. It could be an ancestor of yours that harmed you as a child, an overly critical boss, an ex-lover or a spell caster. This one usually throws them for a quite a loop without harming them.

Lie down flat on your back. Close your eyes and cross your hands over your heart. Breathe deeply. Now imagine there is a pinpoint of light right at your solar plexus. Keep breathing in until this pinpoint of light swells to the size of a glowing yellow star. Now each time you take a breath, imagine this glowing yellow star sending a stream of energy to another pinpoint of light. This light is in your heart. Right now it is enclosed inside the bud of a flower. Each time you take a breath imagine the petals of this flower unfolding to disclose a rose-colored gem in the center.

Imagine this rose-colored light glowing brighter with each breath. As you breathe in, it emanates a warm pink glow about three feet around your body.

For further protection, visualize the entire room you are in filled with this brilliant, rosy pink light. If you concentrate hard enough, you can project this pink light to encompass a whole city block. Project it as far as you can. Surround yourself, your room and your house with this bubble of pink light.

Now visualize the person you suspect of attacking you standing before you. What kind of look does the person have? Is he frowning or scowling? Change that look to a soft smile. Change it to a broad smile. Change it to a look that means that he or she is overjoyed to see you. Scan the person's body with your imagination. Find the heart.

Now breathing deeply, concentrate on sending him a ray of soft, rose-colored light. Send it directly to the heart, for as long as you can. When you feel an inner 'click' inside, stop sending the light.

Now smile at the person and wave goodbye. Say "Bless You" in your mind. Tell her you wish her all the happiness she deserves. Visualize the person turning away from you and waving goodbye. Focus now on your own heart. Concentrate on the petals of the flower. Picture this flower closing over the gem in your heart's center.
Now as you breathe in, concentrate once again on the light in your solar plexus. Imagine this light spreading through your entire body and filling it with gold.

When you are satisfied that your body is filled with gold, say the words "Peace Be Still" and open your eyes.

Soul-to-Soul Talk

This meditation involves having a heart-to-heart talk with another individual's soul. If a person is filled with hate, resentment, fear or envy or has a dysfunctional personality, sometimes it is easy for you to talk to his or her Higher Self rather than to talk in person. The Higher Self is devoid of the same characteristics that the personality has, yet it has a subtle influence on the personality. Using this meditation may manifest a sudden change of behavior on the part of the other person with regards to you. It is useful for all forms of attack.

Lie down your flat on your back. Breathe and relax. Imagine a bright ball of light about three feet above your head. You can actually imagine a being that looks somewhat like you. This is your Higher Self or soul. This is a benevolent, compassionate version of yourself. This is the self that lives in a perfect world. Greet your Higher Self. Imagine your Higher Self smiling and sending you love.

Now imagine another light. This one is hundreds of feet above you. It looks like a burning ball aflame...a small shining sun. It is the purest, whitest light imaginable. This is the Divine Light—the ultimate source of all love and imagination.

As you breathe in, imagine this Divine Light shooting light downwards and sending it into the ball of light that is just above your head. As you breathe out, see your Higher Self being energized by the light sent from this higher sun.

Now imagine the person that you are having problems with. Visualize him or her from head to toe. Imagine this person is standing right in front of you. Now visualize that this person too, has a little ball of shining light about three feet above his or her head.

Now you are going to create a triangle of light. You are going to imagine that there is a beam of light connecting your Higher Self to the other person's Higher Self. Once you have made this connection, you ask that your Higher Self be allowed to speak to the other person's Higher Self. The person is still facing you. Say what it is you have to say. Explain why the hatred or difference between you needs to be dissolved.

Explain why it would be good for you both and everyone else. Keep your words positive: "I would like you to leave me alone because by focusing on me you are reducing your chances of meeting another person."

Now imagine that the shining sun high above you is sending light down to both of your Higher Selves. In your mind's eye you are seeing two people with a triangle of light above both of your heads. The Divine Light is at the top of the triangle.

You ask the Divine Light to send both of you the love, courage, strength and imagination required to resolve the situation.

Keep up this visualization of the Higher Sun sending light down upon both of you for as long as you can. Remember to keep up the image of the energy flowing back and forth between the two of you at the same time.

When you feel you have sent enough energy, you usually feel a little "click" indicating the matter is done. Dissolve the image and open your eyes.

Transmutation Breath

This is a breathing exercise that I use quite a bit with clients to purify the aura, clear the chakras and release any negative energies that might be attached to someone.

You may do this sitting, standing up or lying down. Imagine yourself surrounded in a bubble of golden light. Breathe deeply from your solar plexus.

Close your mouth. Breathe in with both nostrils. As you breathe imagine that you are inhaling Divine Yellow Light. Open your mouth slightly. Hold your breath for a few seconds, allowing this Divine Light to enter every pore of your body, clearing and pushing-out all the negative energy.

As you breathe out through your mouth, imagine all negativity, tension, resentment, sickness and emotions leaving your body. The breath from your exhalation might seem charcoal-colored, foggy or black. The moment this dark breath hits the air, imagine it immediately transformed into shining droplets of shimmering gold.

Do this at least ten times.

The Violet Flame

Saint Germain has given us the Violet Flame and it is a wonderful way to cleanse and clear your aura, your home, your property, even your vehicle. Working with the Violet Flame is very similar to the Burning Flame technique. You can visualize the beautiful violet flames begin at your feet, swirling up and around you, burning off anything in your aura that doesn't belong or that you no longer need.

Another way that we work with the Violet Flame visualization is by invoking the Violet Flame Decree. Say this quickly over and over as you go through your visualization, allowing the flame to burn-off negativity from your aura, each chakra, the room that you're in, the building, you get the idea. The Violet Flame Decree:

"I AM a being of Violet Fire, I AM the purity God desires."

Another Violet Flame Decree that's extremely effective:

HARNESS THE POWER OF THE LIGHT

I AM the violet flame In action in me now
I AM the violet flame To Light alone I bow
I AM the violet flame In mighty cosmic power
I AM the light of God Shining every hour
I AM the violet flame Blazing like a sun
I AM God's sacred power Freeing every one

8

Shielding – The why's & how's?

You should practice psychic protection techniques at least once or twice a day until your body picks up the habit and begins to naturally reinforce your shields with energy. After a month or two you should be proficient enough that you only need to re-visualize your shields once a week. If you find yourself in a particularly nasty situation where you need an extra amount of protection, feel free to shield yourself again even if you had done so earlier in the day. As you become more comfortable and skilled at these techniques you will find it possible to reinforce your shield with little concentration and even while your body is in motion or otherwise distracted.

The psychic shield can be varied to suit your own personal experiences, depending on the type of visualization techniques that you use. Please note that energy for these shields can be drawn from different sources, including the earth itself. Proper shielding techniques should be one of the cornerstones of any psychic training. The techniques are so simple almost any beginner can perform them and are they can be easily mastered with a little practice. Please don't be afraid to experiment with the techniques until you find one that works well for you.

If you feel you are not grounded in your body, and under attack from psychic forces, take your mind off psychic things and concentrate on the most mundane, ordinary things you can think of. If it is dark, put electric lights on. Have a good substantial meal. Many spiritual people live on salads and other very light food, which is good, but there are times when you need something more dense and solid to eat. Watch some light comedy or whatever diverts you, but avoid dark shows about crime and other evils. Whatever you give attention to increases in your world. Avoid alcohol and drugs (unless medically prescribed). In this way you make yourself unavailable until you feel properly grounded and able to cope.

It is very important to live fully in the physical world as well as having adventures in other worlds. After all, we were born here. Anyone who wants to make spiritual progress has to be good at ordinary life. Paying attention to the demands of worldly life helps protect us from unwanted interference.

Many people open their chakras during a meditation and then forget to close them. There are many ways to do this, and one I use is to pass the palm of my right hand over my chakras, starting from the lowest and going up to the crown chakra and over my head, saying: "I ask for these energies to be sealed in the Name of the Christ." You don't need to say this aloud if other people are present.

Strong emotions can hit the solar plexus chakra and cause one to lose energy. If you feel in danger of this happening, you can protect yourself by asking for the Great Sun Disc to be placed over your solar plexus (or anywhere else for that matter.) This is a visualization of the sun and is extremely powerful once you have made an inner connection with it.

You can avoid a lot of problems simply by seeing danger ahead and avoiding it. Sounds obvious, doesn't it. For instance, avoid being drawn into arguments, including long-winded intellectual arguments, which can steal an enormous amount of energy and which you are not likely to win. Sometimes a companion is simply draining your energy and you will end up exhausted, having wasted valuable time as well.

Working With a Competent Energy or Light Worker

First of all, you can and should take care of as much of this on your own as you possibly can. Secondly, if you are convinced that you are absorbing negative energies or are the recipient of psychic attacks, you should contact an Energy or Light Worker for assistance. It's important to work with someone who is experienced in the identification, clearing and elimination of dark energies, entities and spirits. Just because someone read a book on the internet doesn't make them a master of anything. Work with someone who has a proven track record… someone who is highly ethical and professional. This way, you're not being attacked twice.

If you believe that spirits, entities or dark energies have penetrated your body or aura, you should seek out someone legitimate to assist you as soon as possible. It's important to identify and eliminate these entities as soon as possible – but you need to know how to do this safely, as there is a strong possibility that you could draw more negative energies to yourself if you attempt the clearing yourself. This would only exacerbate the situation.

A proficient energy worker can and will protect not only you, but themselves and everyone involved. They will not allow these energies to attack them and will be able to successfully remove anything that is affecting you.

There is no "one-sure-fire" technique to removing these physical attacks. It depends on their strength, whether it is accidental or intentional, if it's a curse or spell, and the strength of the person who has sent this energy along with the strength of the one who has absorbed it.

Last of all, talk to the energy worker before you have a session, to get a feel for their fees and procedures. There are a lot of charlatans out there who charge excessive fees, make the victim come back numerous times or require them to purchase expensive amulets or talismans. If someone is requiring all of these things… keep looking for someone who is more interested in helping than making a profit off of you. Fortunately this new influx of energy coming to earth no longer holds a foundation for false prophets, self-proclaimed gurus and fraudulent psychics. These people are now being brought forth into the light for everyone to clearly see who and what they are.

Find someone who you not only feel comfortable with, but who has your genuine interests at heart. That's why we're called Light Workers! If they don't volunteer the information (which they should), ask them to provide you with information and techniques to protect yourself in this particular situation. If they are worthy of the name Light Worker, they will help empower you to protect yourself.

Whether you decide to consult a professional or not, it is important for you to remember that ultimately you are in charge of your reality, what you believe and think, and your spiritual accountability before God. If it is any comfort, the human aura, like the human body, tends to want to heal rather than destroy itself and most of us have the capability of healing ourselves by looking within and cleaning up our own internal landscapes. Just as "you are what you eat," you are also what you think. If you think you are powerless over astral events in your life, then you will be. If you think only the local shaman has the power to cure you of your ailment, then that will probably come true.

You do not necessarily need a third party to clear you of an astral invasion or an attachment. The most that a Healer or Light Worker can do is try to show you a way out of the darkness. The actual Light is within you, not from an external source. A strong belief in this concept is grandly life affirming and helps you strengthen your aura on the spot.

Historically, there are some tools that have been used to diagnose invasions, attachments and attacks. The most popular one is the pendulum. A pendulum is a chain or rope with a gemstone or cone-shaped piece of metal dangling from the end. The pendulum is passed over the patient's body to look for disturbed energy centers that might be the place of origin of the attack. Traditionally, if the pendulum swings in a counter-clockwise circle as opposed to a clockwise circle then there is a weakness in the energy field in that spot.

Some Reiki or Light Workers may also use psychometry. Stones or crystals are placed on the patient's body and examined later for clarity and temperature to see if the person's energy field is fogged or weak. A Reiki Master may also sense what is going on simply by passing his hands through your energy field. Other individuals may be able to see the obstruction in your aura and remove it using an *anthame* (a ritual knife), their hands or minds.

Kirlian or electromagnetic photography can also be used to take a Polaroid or photograph of your aura. I have found this technology to be the most efficient and practical way to diagnose an aura that is being pulled at or interfered with by another. Spirits in this kind of photography often show up as balls or clusters of light. Attachments or invasions can look like dark spots or pale patches. A healthy aura shows a thin membrane around its bubble of light. In damaged people this membrane is often broken and sometimes even non-existent. Much can be told also by the aura's shape. If it is too conical and tall, it may indicate an attack on the crown chakra. Auras that are too flat, truncated, shifted to one side or missing the symmetry that is associated with a healthy etheric shield are also indications of invasion, damage or astral attack.

9

Additional Methods of Protection you probably never thought of!

Crystals and gemstones

Much has been written about crystals and their protective and supportive properties. We wear them unconsciously when we're about to have a difficult day or important meeting. Crystals can help us not only feel stronger, they actually deflect and filter negativity and ill intentions… removing them and the person from your immediate presence.

This is my personal preference for clearing and protecting a space, probably because I do so much with crystals, but mostly because I've seen how quickly, easily and efficiently they work.

I have a family member who loves nothing better than to verbally attack and publically humiliate certain other family members, myself included. She's not concerned with the truth, she'll say whatever harmful, mean, nasty thing she can think of – just to get her "thrill". Admittedly, this is a very troubled soul and we've tried to help her over the years, but she refuses to acknowledge what she does or accept assistance.

The only other alternative is to protect and shield ourselves when she's around. At one family gathering, there wasn't any way I was going to be able to avoid her, so I decided to wear a gemstone necklace I had just purchased. It's a powerful one… a Herkimer Diamond with a very large Moldavite. This necklace can make some people buzz or even become nauseous, but since I work with high-vibrational stones all the time, it feels like an old friend… and it probably is!

I wore this pendant to the family gathering, and knowing that I would have to face this person, I decided to get it over with as soon as I arrived. I went up to her, said hello and chatted about the weather or something similar – but she couldn't wait to get away from me. I was nice, cordial, even polite, but she couldn't tolerate the energy of that stone. I wore it again at another family gathering about two years later, with even better results. She not only stayed about 20 yards away from me, but her negativity and unpleasant energy was never able to permeate my shields. I wish I'd known about this stone 20-30 years ago!

HARNESS THE POWER OF THE LIGHT

Selecting Your Crystals

Working with crystals will help accelerate your progress along your spiritual path and each stone is a personal selection.

When choosing your crystals or stones, I believe that it's important to go with your first impressions and what feels right to you. Sometimes they even will select you and appear at the right time in your life. If you are purchasing crystals in a shop – close your eyes, take a deep breath, then open your eyes and select the first crystal you see. Keep in mind that size does not matter when it comes to crystals – some of the strongest ones might be very small.

If you are choosing a stone for someone else, keep them in your thoughts as you choose the crystals on their behalf.

THEN you can go for the descriptions and learn about areas where they are most effective. Listen to your inner voice or choose what appeals to you first and most. The logical/ego part doesn't always give us the stones we really need. Use your intuition – it will lead you to what you need to do.

Cleansing Crystals

It's important to cleanse and recharge your crystals on a regular basis, beginning with the moment you get them. Crystals pick-up energy from people or places that they come in contact with, therefore, they should always be cleared before you begin wearing or using them –

you don't know where they've been. Even when I receive crystals from my mentor, I cleanse them immediately because she mails them to me. Just like the rest of the Universe – everything is energy and energy doesn't differentiate between positive or negative. Therefore, if crystals are in a negative atmosphere, chances are that they'll pick-up and hold that negative energy, so we need to diffuse that immediately.

If you use your crystals regularly or on or around other people, you'll need to cleanse and recharge them to help boost their energy. When I use my laser wand – for myself or others – I'll recharge it several times a week to keep it cleared and charged with as much positive, healing energy as possible.

There are no hard and fast rules for cleansing and recharging your stones – once a month should be more than sufficient. It all depends on how much you use your crystals and what they're exposed to.

Most crystals can be cleared by smudging with sage or cedar; putting them in bright sunlight or under a full moon; or burying them in the earth. Some sources also recommend putting the stones next to plants, in dried herbs, with other stones or in either mineral or salt water. Cleansing your crystals will help purify them of positive ions which may have accumulated.

The safest way to recharge white or clear stones is by placing them outside on a glass tray, in bright sunlight between noon and 1 pm. This is the most powerful time of day, according to the Angels and it does an excellent job of clearing and recharging most clear stones.

Others (Amethyst, Fluorite, Rose Quartz) like being placed outside under a full or new moon. I leave these stones out overnight.

If you're unable to place your stones outside, you can put them in a windowsill in view of the sun/moon.

Crystals to protect your energy field
Wearing appropriate crystals keeps your aura strong, helps you feel secure internally and creates a calm space around you.

Crystals can be carried in your pocket, gridded around your home or worn around your neck but remember to cleanse and dedicate crystals before use and cleanse frequently afterwards.

Clear Quartz is one of the most useful energy enhancement tools and the easiest stone to program. It replenishes and restores your aura. Holding Clear Quartz in front of your navel restores and re-energises the energy field around you. Just holding a Clear Quartz expands your energy by 30%.

Most black crystals like Smoky Quartz, Apache Tears or Black Tourmaline keep your energy field clear when you are in a negative environment by absorbing negative or polluting vibes.

Labradorite not only not only safeguards your physical and subtle energies but also attracts spiritual energies to you.

There is much traditional lore surrounding gems and semi-precious stones. Many of them have links with celestial beings and will magnetize their help. Angels and Cosmic Beings wear a many jewels and these jewels have great significance. The list is too long to go into here, but it is good to know that Rose Quartz amplifies love and that Black Tourmaline will soak up negative energies. If you are suffering from psychic attack get hold of a piece of Black Tourmaline and keep it with you.

Metals

Traditional lore will often show you what metals to use and what to avoid. Among metals gold is supreme because it represents the sun and Divine Intelligence. This spiritual value is the reason why people fall back on gold in times of financial crisis. Gold not only has an abiding monetary value but it is also good for your health if you wear it and has been used as a medicine. Divine Beings wear gold. If you cannot afford to buy gold the color gold will also work as an uplifting and protective feature, because it is in the same vibration. The symbol of something is actually the thing itself on another level.

Silver is lunar, so in terms of psychic protection does not have the same value as gold. This may be the place to mention silver or aluminum foil. Silver foil used to be recommended in books on nuclear warfare to protect radios from electromagnetic interference. It also protects from harmful psychic vibrations. If for some reason you have some questionable object in the house - perhaps you have dug up some archaeological curiosity which may carry an ancient curse - wrap it up in silver foil. Better still get rid of it, but in such a way that it will do no harm to anyone else.

Scents

Like music, scent can have a powerful effect on energies and certain scents can create or destroy atmosphere. There is very little in the psychic realm that can withstand a strong disinfectant - however, this is also true of humans!

Garlic and onions are old favorites in the war on hostile psychic influences, and the pungent smell of garlic is said to drive away vampires as well as witches. If you leave cloves of garlic or raw onions lying about, having dedicated them to the task of absorbing negative influences, they are said to be very effective, and you should burn them afterwards if they have been used in this way. Not everyone can live like this, and if you want angels to visit your house you should spare them the onions and garlic.

Clean, fresh smells such as pine or lemon are unpopular with the demonic hordes. Conversely, you should avoid heavy, sensual perfumes such as patchouli.

Roses have always symbolized Divinity. Certain types of mystical experience involve the scent of roses, and Mary and St Therese of Lisieux frequently use roses in their appearances. St Therese is always depicted with an armful of roses. If you are able to have roses in your house or garden you can create a focus for the divine and this in itself will help drive out evil influences.

Best of all are lavender and chamomile. You can put drops of lavender oil on your upper chakras before going to sleep, for additional protection. It can be used all the time as well as drinking chamomile tea. If you don't like the taste of chamomile tea you can mix it with honey or vanilla to make it more palatable. Apparently chamomile can be smelt on the skin if you drink enough of it, and the demonic forces don't like it at all.

Music

Music has the power to change the vibrations of a place completely and immediately. Its psychological effects, for better or worse, are amazing. If you are experiencing psychic bombardment, one of the most efficient means you can use to combat it is to play the right kind of music night and day on a loop until the evil vibration is defeated. You don't have to listen to the music if you don't want to; it can be playing softly in an empty room or even in a cupboard. It can be so soft that you can barely hear it. Its beneficial effects will continually pour out to the world at large.

Music to counteract witchcraft or ghoulish attack must be strongly spiritual and positive in tone. Certain pieces of music were divinely inspired - Handel's *Messiah* for instance is said to have been inspired by the Archangel Raphael - and to play such music is to make contact instantly, if you so desire, with angels and great heavenly beings.

If you are suffering psychic attack, keep away from rock, rap, hip-hop, the blues, jazz and any music which encourages disintegration.

Music that heals is integrative. The following are suggestions of music to play if you are under psychic attack, or would just like something uplifting:

Handel	*Messiah, especially the Hallelujah Chorus*
Beethoven	*Ninth Symphony, esp. the last movement, the Ode to Joy*
Wagner	*Overture to Tannhauser and the Pilgrims Chorus*
Vivaldi	*New World Symphony, Four Seasons*

The above are mighty spiritual affirmations, full of joy and positivity. Below are some more suggestions:

J S Bach	*Toccata and Fugue in D Minor*
	Mass in B Minor
	Passacaglia and Fugue in C Minor

Mozart	*Jupiter symphony, No, 41*
	anything by Mozart is wonderful for raising vibrations
Beethoven	*Symphonies; Emperor Piano Concerto*
Sibelius	*Finlandia*
J Strauss	*Blue Danube and other waltzes*
Wagner	*Prelude to Parsifal Act 1, Tannhauser: Evening Star*
Schubert	*Ave Maria*
Verdi	*Triumphal March from Aida*
Pacbel	*Canon in E Minor*

This is only a short list, and a good collection of hymns, Christmas carols or Gregorian chant would also serve. New Age pieces, as well as meditation or attunement songs are also extremely beneficial. The Ho' oponopono is an excellent song to play on a continuous loop if you're concerned about negative energies. Whenever I have a healing session, I play the Ho' oponopono in the room as I'm preparing for the client. It helps clear the air so that when I invoke Sacred Space, everything is ready.

10

The Power of the Spoken Word

If music has power, so has the spoken word. In earlier times our words had more power than they have today, when they have been so cheapened. The Word is the power by which the Universe was created: "In the beginning was the Word." When it is combined with intent, with visualization and concentration the spoken word still has great power. We have been conditioned not to use the power of the word and people still can find it embarrassing to raise their voice and use it as a tool. Once this inhibition has been overcome, however, there is an enormous range of mantras and invocations available for our use.

Chanting is an extremely powerful way to make changes in your body and your life. It doesn't have to be anything complicated, loud or long, but the vibration of the sounds within your body will help balance your chakras and strengthen your aura almost immediately.

Om Mani Padme Hum

This is my "go-to" prayer, the beautiful Buddhist mantra *Om mani padme hum*. Although it's Buddhist in origin, this mantra is used the world over by millions of people. His Holiness, the Dalai Lama's teachings regarding this mantra are as follows:

> It is very good to recite the mantra *Om mani padme hum*, but while you are doing it, you should be thinking on its meaning, for the meaning of the six syllables is great and vast… The first, *Om*, symbolizes the practitioner's impure body, speech and mind; they also symbolize the pure exalted body, speech and mind of a Buddha. The path is indicated by the next four syllables. *Mani*, meaning jewel, symbolizes the factors of method – the altruistic intention to become enlightened, compassion and love. The two syllables *padme*, meaning lotus, symbolize wisdom. Purity must be achieved by an indivisible unity of method and wisdom, symbolized by the final syllable *hum*, which indicates indivisibility.

The usual translation of *Om mani padme hum* is "The jewel is in the lotus." Using the Dalai Lama's meanings, it can be translated as "The body, the gemstone, and wisdom are inseparable."

I have found that by reciting this mantra and by listening to a beautiful rendition by Buddhist Monks, I can pull myself out of even the most difficult of moods. If I'm working on a client, who appears to have quite a few "issues", I'll repeat this beautiful chant in my mind while I'm giving a healing session. It quite simply works miracles.

Prayers for Protection

As children, most of us were taught to say our prayers before each meal and when we went to bed. Of course, there were always lots of prayers spoken during religious services, but I've noticed that quite often, we weren't really taught how to pray.

The Bible gave us some of the most beautiful examples of prayers and we should use them as we feel guided.

As with anything spiritual, it's not the spoken words that are important, but the intent. It's not necessary to quote any or all of these prayers perfectly, but it is important to feel, to believe, and to know deep in your heart that you are and will be protected at all times by God and His Angels. All you have to do is take a few minutes and simply ask for his protection and guidance.

The Lord's Prayer

Our Father which art in heaven, Hallowed be thy name.

Thy kingdom come, Thy will be done in earth, as it is in heaven.

Give us this day our daily bread.

And forgive us our debts, as we forgive our debtors.

And lead us not into temptation, but deliver us from evil: For thine is the kingdom, and the power, and the glory, for ever. Amen".

The 23rd Psalm

The Lord *is* my shepherd; I shall not want.
He maketh me to lie down in green pastures: he leadeth me beside the still waters.

He restoreth my soul: he leadeth me in the paths of righteousness for his name's sake.

Yea, though I walk through the valley of the shadow of death, I will fear no evil: for thou *art* with me; thy rod and thy staff they comfort me.

Thou preparest a table before me in the presence of mine enemies: thou anointest my head with oil; my cup runneth over.

Surely goodness and mercy shall follow me all the days of my life: and I will dwell in the house of the Lord for ever. Amen.

The Serenity Prayer

God grant me the serenity
To accept the things I cannot change;
Courage to change the things I can;
And wisdom to know the difference.

Living one day at a time;
Enjoying one moment at a time;
Accepting hardships as the pathway to peace;
Taking, as He did, this sinful world
As it is, not as I would have it;
Trusting that He will make all things right
If I surrender to His Will;
So that I may be reasonably happy in this life
And supremely happy with Him
Forever and ever in the next.

Amen.

The Unity Prayer

> The Light of God surrounds me.
> The Love of God enfolds me.
> The Power of God protects me.
> The Presence of God watches over me.
> The Mind of God guides me.
> The Life of God flows through me.
> The Laws of God direct me.
> The Power of God abides within me.
> The Joy of God uplifts me.
> The Strength of God renews me.
> The Beauty of God inspires me.
> Wherever I am, God is!

Prayers to Archangel Michael for Intercession and Protection

Glorious St. Michael, guardian and defender of the Church of Jesus Christ, come to my assistance, against whom the powers of hell are Unchained. Guard with special care me, my family, my home, animals and my business. Protect all the beautiful souls and especially the children.

St. Michael, watch over us, defend us against the assaults of the demon, and assist us especially against the dark and negative energies who attack us now. Help us achieve the happiness of beholding God face to face for all eternity.

St. Michael, intercede for me with God in all my necessities, especially protection from negative energies and intent that is being sent in my direction. Help my life to flourish so that I may help and teach others about your loving, healing energy. Give me strength to follow my path, so that I may help spread your light and love throughout the Universe.   (add anything you'd like to this portion of the prayer)

Obtain for me a favorable outcome in the matters I recommend to you. Mighty Prince of the heavenly host, and victor over rebellious spirits, remember me and keep me grounded, safe and on my path. Be for me, I pray, my powerful aid in temptation and difficulty, and above all do not forsake me in my struggle with the powers of evil. Amen.

11

Meeting Your Guides & Protectors

We all have Spirit Guides, Protectors, Guardian Angels… whatever you want to call them and they've got your back!

There's nothing like working with your Guardian Angels, Spirit Guides, and Protectors! Having these powerful beings around you helps protect against negative thought forms and psychic attack. Everyone has them and all we need to do is learn to call on them for protection in our times of need.

Many people want to use Archangel Michael as their Protector, but are afraid to call on him. He's God's Warrior Angel – ready with his sword to smite down anyone who causes harm. Michael is the Right Hand of God, so there's no one better to call on to protect you. Don't worry or think that by calling on Michael that you're taking him away from someone who "really needs him". He is omnipresent… meaning he's everywhere at once and certainly capable of taking care of each one of us at any given time.

Working with Angels, Ascended Masters, Saints and Guides

Where would we be without our Angels, Ascended Masters and Spirit Guides? Most of us would probably have been gone a long time ago… myself included. Mine have interceded during a F-4 tornado and a horrific auto crash. If it wasn't for their help, this book would never have been written and I wouldn't have worked with and healed 1,000's of people. Our Angels (et al) are here to guide and protect us. Most people just think of them as being Guardian Angels, saving us from all sorts of difficulties, but they're really much more than that.

The definition of 'Angel' is a celestial or non-physical being, who is an egoless messenger of God. Angels and Archangels are God's chosen helpers. Most people have two Guardian Angels, while some can have more, depending on what they need at any given time. You can receive more Guardian Angels if either you or someone else requests them for you. These are your personal angels, who are with you from birth. They assisted you in your decision to come to Earth and they will help you all along the way, for your entire life. Your Guardian Angels love you unconditionally and only want the best for you. They never get tired, or bored or frustrated… they're with you no matter what happens.

We don't pray to or worship our Angels, however it is their job to do God's will, whatever that may be for each of our lives. We've been told that they're not allow to intercede in a situation, until we ask for their help. Although God and the Angels always know what it is that we want and need, it is still up to us to ask for their assistance. The Divine Law decrees that they are not allowed to interfere with our 'free will' unless we specifically ask for their help. Sometimes I believe that the Angels might be a little guilty of 'stepping in' before they've been asked, in situations such as auto accidents or, in my case, an F-4 tornado. I didn't have time to stop for a prayer, but I know, without a doubt that my life was saved that day by my Angels – and I'm very glad they interceded for me.

As wonderful as our Guardian Angels are, remember that they are Celestial Beings who have never lived on Earth before. Sometimes when we're praying and talking to them, we need to remember that it's important to ask them for their assistance… without giving them step-by-step instructions on what to do. I've found that things work best when I ask for "the greatest and highest benefits for all concerned" or something similar. Once you ask for assistance for everyone involved – no matter what the situation is – things generally turn out much better than I anticipated.

There are nine Choirs or levels of Angels, in addition to Angels who have specialties, all designed to help us through our journey:

- ∞ ***Seraphim:*** These are the highest order of Angels, who are said to be shining brightest, as they are the closest to God. They are pure light.

- ∞ ***Cherubim:*** Usually portrayed as chubby children with wings, these are the second-highest order of Angels. They are pure love.

- ∞ ***Thrones:*** The triad of Seraphim, Cherubim and Thrones resides in the highest realms of Heaven. Thrones are the bridge between the material and the spiritual, and represent God's fairness and justice.

- ∞ ***Dominions:*** These Angels are the highest in the next triad level of Angels. They are the overseers or managers of Angels, according to God's will.

- ∞ ***Virtues:*** These Angels govern the order of the physical universe, watching over the sun, moon, stars, planets and Earth.

- ∞ ***Powers:*** Powers are peaceful warriors who purify the Universe from lower energies.

- ∞ ***Principalities:*** The third triad consists of the Angels closest to the Earth. The Principalities watch over the planet, including nations and cities, to ensure God's will of peace on Earth.

- ∞ ***Archangels:*** This choir comprises the overseers of humankind and of the Guardian Angels. Each Archangel has a specialty representing an aspect of God.

- ∞ ***Guardian Angels:*** Each person on this Earth has Guardian Angels assigned to him or her throughout life.

Many of these Angels have names and while in meditation, you can always ask to find out the names of those who are with you. However, there are also very many Angels who do not have specific names. I've found that sometimes people get too 'hung-up' on the names of their Angels… like one is better than another. That can't be further from the truth!

I know that often I receive messages from the Angels and instead of focusing on who's delivering the message… I focus on receiving the message correctly. When I receive these messages and don't have a specific Angel attached to the message, I've been directed to say that the message was channeled from the Angels of Light. As long as it's Divinely inspired… they're all excellent messengers.

Ascended Masters are different from Angels in that they have lived on the Earth, but have learned all the lessons they needed to and ascended back into Heaven. They have raised their vibration to a sustained frequency of light and can come and go at will from the earth plane without the birth/death cycle. They were great spiritual teachers and healers, and are now powerful guides who can help us as we go through our lives. They, too, can be our protectors and guides – working alongside our Guardian Angels.

Each Ascended Master has specialties such as healing, manifesting, ascension, relationships, protection, you name it. They come from every religion and culture and are non-denominational. Like the Angels, they are always here to lend a hand, however we may need it, whether it's learning about our life purpose or helping to protect us from negativity or attacks. They've been here, they know what we're dealing with, and they're here to help. There are many recognized Ascended Masters, and I've discovered, quite a few that are extraordinary who haven't "made the list". My own personal Guardian/Protector is an Ascended Master, although you'd never find his name listed anywhere. He lived in early Byzantine times and was assigned the duties of watching over me that far back. He's one of the Logos – which according to Catholic teachings is the term by which Christian theology in the Greek language designates the Word of God, or Second Person of the Blessed Trinity. He's been a quiet presence until recently, while he's now busy helping me get the word out, so that I can reach and help more people. He reappeared in my life just after I received the message that I was to dramatically expand my reach and serve even more people.

The Ascended Masters have worked with mankind throughout the centuries. Most of the time in the past the Ascended Masters have worked in the background. There were some Ascended Masters who have assisted mankind such as Sanat Kumara. also known in the Bible as the "Ancient of Days", by some He is known as the "Lord of the World".

Sanat Kumara came ages ago to give assistance to the Earth when it would have been dissolved otherwise. He offered His own free will to supply the Light required to sustain the Earth and keep the Earth in the system until enough so mankind could be raised to a point where they could carry the responsibility of emitting sufficient Light.

Ascended Master Saint Germain's Cosmic Name is "Freedom". He is the Cosmic Father of the people of America. Saint Germain's work for the freedom of mankind began in that civilization seventy thousand years ago; when a whole civilization could have been raised into the Ascension had they continued to give obedience instead of becoming rebellious.

Following are some of the commonly recognized Ascended Masters:

> ***Jesus Christ:*** The Son of God. Because of his incarnation on the Earth, he is considered to be the Son of God and an Ascended Master.
>
> ***Mother Mary:*** The young woman who agreed to bring Jesus into the world.

Mary Magdalene: The wife of Jesus and the "Disciple of the Disciples". She was a powerful force in the early Christian movement and is the author of the Gospel of Mary and other spiritual writings.

Saint Germain: He is the bringer of the age of Aquarius and comes bearing the gift of the Violet Flame for world change. He tutors and initiates souls in mastery of the seat-of-the-soul chakra, preparing them to receive the Holy Spirit's gifts of prophecy and the working of miracles.

El Morya: He was thought to originally been the embodiment of Abraham of the Old Testament.

Lanto: An ancient Chinese master who lived around 400 BC. He is said to have accomplished more than any other master of earth.

Paul the Venetian: An Italian Master Renaissance painter and spiritual revolutionary who saw beauty as the most powerful catalyst for enlightenment.

Serapis Bey: An Ascended Master associated with Luxor in Egypt, who holds open the Temple doors on the etheric level and is one of the great teachers of ascension on the planet.

Hilarion: He is connected with the Temple of Truth and is helping to bring in the scientific aspect of the New Age.

Lady Master Nada: A beautiful Ascended Master who is said to be the twin flame of Jesus Christ. She works with mental healing, upliftment, and enlightenment for the feminine.

Maha Chohan: Referred to as "The Comforter", he was with the Disciples ten days after Jesus' ascension. He draws and supplies the energy used in all nature and by mankind.

Kuthumi: He has worked with Archangel Jophiel and helps to touch people with wisdom and illumination, tact, foresight, consideration and friendliness.

Babaji: He is the immortal master of the Himalayas, known as the deathless avatar. After ascension he promised to stay in his physical body to help all humanity.

Melchizedek: An ancient Cosmic Being who holds the secrets of God, the Universe and the true history of the planet.

Sanat Kumara: He has assisted humanity from the lighter realms, possibly longer than any other master.

Quan Yin: The great goddess and Mother of Compassion. Following her ascension she turned back to save others and made a pledge to never enter into final peace alone.

Sri Ramakrishna: One of the most revered and greatest Hindu Saints. Beloved for his great devotion, he taught universal love and understanding of all religions.

Maitreya: Whose name is derived from the Sanskrit maître, meaning Universal Love. He is known to Buddhists as the embodiment of loving kindness.

Hathor: The Goddess Hathor who represents an ascended civilization of the fourth and fifth dimensions. The Hathors are giving loving assistance and profound ascension teachings to humanity and earth.

Yogananda: The Indian yogi who came to America in 1920 and introduced millions to the Eastern ways of enlightenment.

Gautama Buddha: The Buddha was one of the great enlightened ones, teaching detachment and the middle way. He represents the wisdom energy while Christ is the love energy.

Krishna: Born as a cowherd boy, Krishna displayed his perfect divinity with all the attractive features of wealth, power, fame, beauty, wisdom and detachment. He enchanted all with the music of his flute.

Metatron: One of the major Archangels, assigned by God to be in charge of this present Creation. He was Enoch in an earthly incarnation.

Ganesha: The God of Wisdom and Good Fortune and the patron of learning and letters, according to the Hindu religion.

Saint Teresa of Avilia: A sixteenth-century reformer of the Carmelite order in Spain, who often communed with Jesus.

Ramtha: The "Lord of the Wind" was the first human ever to ascend from the earth. He has been at the leading edge of teachings on ascension and enlightenment for the last 25 years thru his exclusive channel, JZ Knight.

Thoth: A demi-god, Thoth is most often depicted as wearing an ibis mask. He was considered by Ancient Egyptians to be the god of the moon, god of wisdom and measurer of time. He was the inventor of writing and numbers, being credited with devising the standard 365-day year.

There are many more Ascended Masters, throughout history, however these are the primary ones that are called upon.

Protective Saints

Appealing to or making a petition to the Saints for assistance against astral attack is a tradition found in Catholicism, Christianity, Wiccan, and New Age religions.

Traditionally, the request is written on a small slip of paper and placed under the burning candle on very specific days of the week. Commercial candles, featuring an image of a Saint on a glass jar filled with wax can be purchased for this purpose. However, it is my opinion that these candle-burning rituals require nothing more than the lighting of the appropriately colored candle and a short, sincere prayer for help that is directly addressed to the Saint.

> *Saint Alex:* On a Sunday, burn a pink candle and ask for protection against negative thought forms and the harm your enemies might wish to send you.
>
> *Saint Barbara:* On a Saturday, light a red candle to ward off all evil, protect against astral interference, clear your path of obstacles and ask for protection against binding or black magic.
>
> *Saint Cipriano:* On a Saturday, light a purple candle and ask for protection from black magic. He also protects against bad neighbors, liars, cheaters, addicts, bad coincidences, man-made disasters and natural disasters.

Saint Clare of Assisi: On a Monday, light a white candle and ask for protection from alcoholics, mentally ill people and psychic invaders. She can also assist you with your own temptations.

Saint Dymphna: On a Monday, light a blue candle to help with obsession, possession by demons, nervous disorders and astral attack from the living or the dead.

Our Lady of Fatima: On a Tuesday, light a white candle and pray for protection from binding situations, spells and evil spirits.

Saint Francis of Assisi: On a Monday, light a brown candle and ask him for protection against secret plots, conspiracies and cults.

Saint Gerard Magella: On a Monday, light a white candle for overall astral protection as well as protection while channeling, healing or practicing mediumship.

Saint Ignatius of Loyola: On a Saturday, light a white candle and ask for assistance in ridding a house of evil spirits, entities or ghosts.

Saint John The Baptist: On a Tuesday, light a green candle and ask for protection from astral enemies or anything or anyone that shakes your faith.

Saint Jude: On any day light green, white and red candles together when trapped in what seems a hopeless or desperate situation.

Saint Lucy of Syracuse: On a Wednesday, light a white candle and ask for temptations to be conquered, obstacles cleared and protection from the evil eye.

Saint Louis Beltran: On any day light a white candle to remove the evil eye from children.

Saint Philomena: On a Saturday, light a pink or green candle and ask this patroness of desperate situations to cleanse you from all evil thought forms and to restore your soul.

Saint Martin Cabalkro: On any day light a red and white candle together to block obstacles and black magic, rescue someone from evil influences or ask for release from demonic possession.

Saint Rita of Cascia: On a Sunday, light a white candle and ask for deliverance from abusive relationships. She also helps restore faith and provides you with patience.

Saint Therese of Lisieux: On a Wednesday, light a yellow candle and petition her for protection against addicts and for protection from harm from enemies using black magic.

Another interesting thing that I've learned about Angels, Ascended Masters, Saints, Personal Guardians and Protectors is that they occasionally rotate. The ones that you need today aren't the same ones that you needed when you were 5 years old. Your Guardian Angels always stay the same, but you have additional team-members that back them up, too. It seems that the saying, "it takes a village to raise a child" applies to all of us… it takes a team of Angels to guide each of us through our journey of life.

Most people would like to know who their Angels, Guides and Protectors are, so that they can have a more personal relationship with them. If you'd like to meet your own Spirit Guide/Protector, the following meditation can assist you in meeting and getting to know each of your own special Guardian Angels:

Meeting Your Personal Guardian/Protector

Take a few minutes to relax and close your eyes. Breathe out any tension you may be feeling – while breathing in a sense of peace and relaxation. Take as long as you need to gradually withdraw your attention from the outside world and into yourself.

Look up to your inner screen and project an image of a place where you feel happy and protected… your own sacred room. This can be an actual place or one from your imagination. Think about this place and it will appear in your mind. Spend a few minutes enjoying that place, remembering how good it feels to be there. Let your senses bring you the smell of this place, its own unique, fragrant perfume. Let your skin show you the warmth of this place. Sense what it's like to be in this beautiful place.

While you are enjoying your special place, know that this is your sacred room – you can come back here at any time to visit, to re-energize yourself, to rest and re-charge. You are always safe here!

As you are standing in this most special place, picture a copper cord running from the bottom of your feet, deep down into the earth. This cord holds you in incarnation. It is flexible, allowing you to move, but is hooked into the core of the earth, anchoring your physical body in everyday reality. With this cord in place, you will always be grounded and centered.

Gradually you'll become aware that there is a shaft of bright light shining down and touching the ground several feet in front of you.

This light pulsates with energy and flashes of color. Behind this beautiful light is a door. You know that there's something very special just on the other side of that door.

As you walk towards this light, you feel a tremendous sense of peace and love coming from it. You hear the sounds of nature, gently surrounding you. You begin to hear music, as if from the heavens, barely audible at first, then softly surrounding you in relaxation and a cocoon of love As you begin to step into this light, the mysterious door opens and you are greeted by someone. This is your Guardian Angel. What does your Guardian look like? Is it a person, spirit or animal? Is your Guardian male or female? What is it wearing?

Welcome your Guardian. Ask what their name is. Spend time getting comfortable with your Guardian, knowing that they will be with you at all times. Ask if you need a sign or symbol that will enable you to call on your Guardian instantly in time of need. Ask them for protection and strength, and that they will be with you, any time you need assistance.

Ask your Guardian if there is anything that they want you to know at this time – if they have any messages or gifts for you. When you have spent enough time with your Guardian, thank them for coming and ask them to be there for you in your time of need.

Switch your attention back into the room, leaving your Guardian safely tucked-away in your inner eye. Check that your cloak of protection is in place and that you are fully occupying your body as you gradually come back to consciousness.

Now that you know who your Guardian/Protector is, you can call on them in times of need. Remember that they're not only here to help you with something catastrophic happens – they can help with that business presentation, homework, relationships… the list is just as endless as their love for you! So… start asking them to be with you. It doesn't always have to be in times of stress, they can accompany you when you commute to work, have an important meeting or presentation, or if you are healing or channeling. Become friends with your Guardian, because there's no better friend to have than a Divine Being assigned to care for you.

12

Protecting your space

Another way to ensure that you are fully protected is to create a safe space to live, work or meditate. Regular smudging, burning incense, drumming, rattling, sprinkling with holy water, etc will keep the psychic air fresh and the vibrations clear. Having flowers and plants is very beneficial, in addition to occasionally opening the windows to let a breeze in and release stagnant air. Having crystals in a room will work wonders for not only soaking-up bad vibrations, but to protect and shield your home and property.

It's important to keep your entire living space clear and protected, but you'll need to pay special attention to the place where you meditate or do other spiritual work. Don't forget to absorb not only the negative energy that comes from the TV, computers and phones, but the electromagnetic radiation, too. This can adversely affect your aura and energy fields and needs to be attended to. No matter how good your personal protection is, if you're in an area that's negative, it's going to drag you down.

Another thing that we need to be mindful of at home is our own psychic energy. First of all, there's the 'stuff' that you bring home from a day at the office and driving in traffic. I can't think of anything positive about that stuff, so when you get in the car to leave work, brush you aura off. This leaves any negativity back at the workplace and not in your car. Always ask your Angels or Guides to take this negative energy to the light to be transmuted – or to Mother Earth to absorb it, cleanse the energy and use it to heal the earth. Either way don't leave your 'stuff' for someone else to 'step in'.

You may think that negative psychic energy isn't something that's tangible, but it is. I've encountered many instances when someone has brushed-off the negativity or watched another healer 'toss' the negative energy away… only to see someone else receive it. In fact, one day I was clearing myself, brushing the negativity off of me and in particular, some that had built-up in my sinus area. I was so busy clearing all this out that I wasn't paying attention to what was going on around me, until it was too late. It seems that as I was brushing and pulling this nasty energy off of me, I slung it on my poor dog, who was laying down asleep next to me. As soon as I threw the energy his way, he jumped-up and ran out of the room! Talk about feeling bad... I had to chase him down so I could do a clearing on him, then he went right back to sleep.

Before you go into your home, after being out in public, brush yourself off – again allowing the negativity to dissolve and be transmuted. Place Black Tourmaline on either side of your door to cleanse and filter any energy you bring into your home. Other crystals that are useful for protection, healing and cleansing are Rose Quartz, Amethyst, Citrine, Selenite, Clear Quartz and Fluorite. Turquoise is always an excellent stone to have in your home or to wear because of its highly protective properties. Having these stones placed either in a group or scattered around the house will help keep the vibrations high and the negativity low. This is also excellent for the office. Not everyone has a large space to display crystals, but even if you have a tiny spot on your desk to place some in a bowl, it'll help clear the area of negativity and EMF radiation and will look pretty at the same time.

Sacred Space is where you spend time in meditation or prayer and this area should be kept extra-clean energetically. Make sure you smudge or burn good quality incense in the space before and during meditations, as well as keeping crystals on your altar. You can also keep a small statue of a protective deity or Guardian Angel on your altar. Burning a candle is also helpful in holding a peaceful sacred space and music is really important. Playing high vibrational or attunement music in your sacred space will lift the vibrational level incrementally and always ensure that your space is cleared.

When arranging your sacred space (or your home or office), check into the principals of Feng Shui to ensure that you are creating the most harmonious environment possible. For instance, if you feel that "bad vibes" are coming from a particular direction, place a mirror on the wall to reflect those energies away from your space. Feng Shui has many principals that are extremely beneficial to arranging your home, office or sacred space. I believe that if someone applies these principals to their decorating, they will benefit tremendously.

All of these things are great once you're in a home – but what do you do when you're relocating to a new apartment, home or office? That's usually when we need to do our most serious cleansing and clearing.

Not everyone has the ability to move into a brand-new location and let's face it, no place is exempt from negative energies, even a new house. You don't know if something traumatic happened on that land 1,000's of years ago or if a contractor smashed his thumb while nailing a board in your house. Even a brand new place can have negative energies and even entities attached, depending on what happened on the land and people who were working on the house.

Homes that have been lived in often have even more issues. The previous families could have had marital problems, there could have been illness or a death in the home. So many homes on the market now are foreclosures, so there's a lot of negative emotional energy residual in the house. The previous occupants could have had drug or alcohol problems, the list of "what if's" goes on forever. Needless to say, when we decide to move into a new home or apartment, we need to do some serious cleansing and clearing before we get settled. All of these places and each of these situations can be cleared out easily so that you won't have to deal with someone else's baggage.

Also, don't let a death prevent you from moving into a new place. I've had homes that were previous foreclosures, one that had one owner (with no drama), and two homes that had deaths… one natural and the other by suicide. I have to say, without a doubt, that the home that had a suicide was the "cleanest" one that I've lived in. In fact, the energy in it is beautiful and has been from the first day we stepped onto the property. You see, the man who died there, couldn't live without his beloved wife, who had passed earlier. His was an act of true love. While I certainly don't condone this and admit that the couple was elderly, I have to say that this home and the surrounding property are magical. Orbs are everywhere you look and the energy is always beautiful. We have gorgeous Rose Quartz boulders everywhere and the place is filled with light and love.

Ironically, the home that I lived in that had one previous owner and no drama ended-up being haunted and I couldn't stand being in it one minute longer. So it doesn't always matter what the history is, it's what you feel when you're in the space and your ability to clear it of negative energies, entities and general nastiness.

These initial cleansings can be fairly easy and extremely potent. You can do it yourself or, if you feel that there is a darkness in the home, you can call on an experienced Light Worker to help clear the area. Either way, this can be accomplished without too much trouble and then you can move into your dream home without being exposed to energies that aren't in your best interests.

The first thing to do when you are looking at the prospective home is to just take some time to sense and feel if anything negative is in the house. If you're with a realtor, ask them to give you a few minutes alone to collect your thoughts, then take some time to simply feel. Are you sensing any energy fields? Are there any areas of the home that are unusually cold? Did you get chills when you stepped into a room? Have you had the feeling that someone is watching as you go through the house? Did you see any shadows flit across corners or doorways as you walked around? If you said yes to any of these things, then your prospective home may already have an occupant. The important question is does this feel 'friendly' or 'evil'? Most of the time it's a friendly presence that just needs some assistance going to the Light.

Once you've decided that this is the home for you, before you move in, take a little time to cleanse and clear the home energetically.

People usually get so excited about moving into a new home, they're more worried about getting those boxes unpacked and furniture arranged than they are about the energetic aspects of the home.

If I were moving into a new home today, I would take a little time to do the following before we started moving in:

1. Go through the house, opening windows to let fresh air in and any left-over spirits out.
2. Say a prayer to God, the Angels, Guides and Protectors to help me cleanse and clear this home of anything that is not in my greatest or highest good.
3. Thoroughly smudge the entire building with sage, inside and out. This includes closets, cabinets, fireplace, and the exterior and outbuildings. If you're in an apartment or condo, you can focus on the interior of your specific space.
4. Sweep the entire house, cleaning it physically and energetically, sweeping anything that is not wanted out the doors and relegating it to the Earth.
5. If you're wanting a little extra 'insurance' in clearing the house, you can use the Triple Grid House Clearing. Ask Archangel Michael to help you with this to ensure that everything is clear and ready for you to move in.

6. If you still feel that you need something extra or that the house isn't entirely clear (which it should be), you can always use the Holy Water Wash. It's really not a bad idea to go ahead and use this periodically, just to make sure that your home is spotless energetically. This is also beneficial if you've had a (human) visitor who has very negative energy or if something negative has happened in the home.
7. Last and certainly not least, say a prayer of thanks to God, the Angels, Guides and Protectors for cleansing and clearing the house and for protecting the new family moving into the home.

Triple Grid Protection for House Clearing

For those "Do it yourself" folks, here is one of the techniques that I use. It is very powerful and effective. Like any spiritual process or technique, approach it in Sacred Space with prayer and intention. You may also burn candles, sage, or incense as you are guided. I also use the Feng Shui technique of playing bells or my Tibetan Singing Bowl to help move energy.

In the Triple Grid Technique, you ask the Angels to set up the level of the protective grid, designating the size and shape. You will want to renew the grid often or whenever you feel the energies getting low or out of sync.

Use the invocation: "Legions of Michael: grid level one, spherical my house. Destroyer Force Angels: grid level two, spherical, my house. Circle Security: grid level three, spherical, my house."

"Destroyer Force Angels, please spin your grid, spinning out astral entities, stray electromagnetic influences, fear, disharmony, anger, adverse astrological influences, expectation, frustration, viruses, fungus, bacteria, worry, astral distortions, miscommunication, sadness, enemy patterning, scarcity, loneliness and spin out anything that hasn't been mentioned in this or any other language, but which you know needs to LEAVE the space at this time."

When the clearing feels complete, continue with: "Reverse the spin, same stuff." When that feels complete, end with: "Stop spin. . Thank you God, thank you Angels, thank you Guides."

"Legions of Michael, infuse your grid with the energies of Grace, Faith, Peace, Purity, Liberty, Harmony and Victory Elohim. Infuse it with love, intimacy, the Unified Chakra, centeredness, clarity, full connection with Spirit, tolerance, clear communication, health, wealth, following Spirit without hesitation, mastery, sovereignty, living Heaven and anything else I haven't mentioned in this or any other language, but which you know needs to be IN the space at this time. Please seal the grid. Thank you God, thank you Angels, thank you Guides."

"Circle Security, realign the grids to harmonize with upper-dimensional grid-works. Release all distortions and parasites on the grids. Infuse frequencies for clearer communication with Spirit. Seal the grid. Thank you God, thank you Angels, thank you Guides."

Holy Water Wash

This is a great way to cleanse either a room or entire house. Begin by obtaining Holy Water from the local Catholic Church. Don't use the online-do-it-yourself stuff. Holy Water is free, just bring a small bottle with you and the church will gladly share theirs with you. You'll also need sea salt, which can be purchased at any grocery store.

Once you have your water and sea salt ready, begin by saying a prayer, asking God and your Angels to help you cleanse and clear the room/house/office of any negativity or entities. Ask that they fill the room with Divine Light and Love. Beginning at the door, go around the room in a clockwise manner, lightly sprinkling the Holy Water around baseboards, in corners, around doors and windows, and around photos or mirrors. As you are sprinkling the water, repeat the Lord's Prayer until you complete the room. Make certain that you include closets and cabinets, as these are great spaces for negative energies to hide.

When this is finished, retrace your steps with the sea salt, leaving a little in each corner, in the closet, on windowsills, etc. This will help protect and keep your room clear of negativity. Continue saying the Lord's Prayer as you do this. You can also include Hail Mary's, if you're so inclined.

After you have thoroughly gone through the room with the Holy Water and sea salt, again say a prayer thanking God and the Angels for cleansing, clearing and protecting you and the room.

Once you've performed these rituals, you new home, apartment or office should be clean, clear and ready for you to move in. If, for any reason, that you still feel that there might be some negative energies or entities in the space, it would probably be best, at this point to contact an experienced Light Worker to assist you in clearing the space.

It's always a good idea to smudge and clear your space on a regular basis. For most people, monthly would be fine, however, if your space is in a toxic area or if someone enters the space who is always negative or toxic, or has issues of drug or alcohol abuse, you'll need to cleanse and clear the area much more often.

13

Ways to Prevent or Stop an Attack

1. There are four Golden Rules that you should always remember:

   (a) Light is always stronger than Darkness.

   (b) Darkness cannot exist where there is Light.

   (c) Love is the most powerful force in the Universe.

   (d) A person of low consciousness cannot harm a person of high consciousness.

   As Gautama Buddha said: *"The fool who does evil to a man who is good, to a man who is pure and free from sin, the evil returns to him like the dust thrown against the wind."*

   Therefore raise your consciousness. Be good. Be kind. Dwell in the Light.

2. Take good care of yourself. Keep your body fit and healthy. Always be positive and cheerful, and don't let your mind become negative and melancholy. The world is beautiful! Life is a gift, enjoy it, be happy!

3. Sacred symbols have tremendous power, and are potent defenses against evil. The two most powerful are:

(a) The Pentagram - a five pointed star symbolizing the four elements, and the fifth, the spirit pointing heavenwards. It also symbolizes the human body.

Satanists wear the Pentagram with the 'head' pointing downwards, representing their opposition to God and the Light. The Pentagram has been a long standing tradition as a symbol of Light, being utilized in both Judaism and Christianity. The beautiful west window in London's Westminster Abbey is the shape of a Pentagram.

(b) The Seal of Solomon - a six pointed star. This is the symbol of God, and it is tremendously uplifting and soul strengthening. The upright triangle represents Love, Truth and Wisdom, the downward represents the World, the Flesh and Darkness.

Overall it is symbolic of life's eternal lesson that *Good will always triumph over Evil.*

Meditate on each of the symbols of sacred geometry and let your soul choose the one most suitable for you.

4. Here are two ways of mentally purging your body of negativity.

(a) On a sunny day go outside and hold your arms up to the sun. Feel yourself bathed in Light and the warmth and comfort of God's love and protection. Picture the golden rays of the sun entering your body, reaching, cleansing and rejuvenating every cell, every atom of your body. As d*arkness cannot dwell where there is light* feel all negativity being forced out of your body leaving you as a pure vessel of Light and Love and Goodness.

(b) Mentally visualize yourself as being on a high mountain in springtime. Picture the mountain, its peak capped with virgin snow; further down, where the sun has melted, pretty alpine flowers are in bloom on the craggy, grassy slopes. The sun is shining, the sky a gorgeous blue, the air is so vitalizing and fresh, it is a beautiful day! A mountain stream meanders its way down the slope of the valley far below. Its waters are crystal clear and as pure as pure can be. Make these images come alive in your mind.

See yourself there on the mountain, visualize, as if by magic, the waters of the mountain stream enter into you, *see* them enter into your head and gradually go down through every part, and every cell, and every atom of your body.

Visualize every bad thing, all the negativity, all the troubling thoughts and any illness within you being washed away. *See* the waters leaving you, by flowing out of your toes, carrying away all the bad things, and leaving only good.

Look below you, see all negativity being swept away from you and disappearing into the distance. Now *look* around you, all is good and pure. You are a new person. You have never felt so good you have never been so free! Rejoice!

5. No psychic attack can harm you if your aura is strong and impregnable. The sealing of the aura is an entirely mental process. This is how to do it:

Imagine yourself as being completely encircled by pure, clear, beautiful and dazzling white light. It covers your body totally, from beneath your feet to above your head and all around your body, forming a protective shell around you.

White Light is the radiation of Spirit, of God and goodness. The White Light is the armor of the soul.

Practice this exercise every day. After a while you will be able to feel the presence and power of your protective aura. You will be protected against all psychic evil.

Note: The White Light aura is the Shield of Faith mentioned in Ephesians 6:16.

6. Take a bath. There's nothing more cleansing and relaxing than a bath with one cup each of sea salt, Epsom salt and baking powder. You can also add a drop or two of lavender and a few candles for atmosphere. This will not only help cleanse and detox your body, but it will help clear your aura of any negative energies that may have tried to attach themselves to you during the day. Showers are also a great way to cleanse and clear the aura. You can use the bath salt mixture as a scrub all over the body if you don't have time for a luxurious bath.

7. If you are psychically attacked *never* fight fire with fire. If you do you will have an inferno on your hands! Douse the flames of hate with the waters of Love. Send forth a blessing to your attacker.

    "Bless them who curse you, pray for them who maltreat you", said Jesus. Such wisdom!

    Your attacker is most likely mentally or spiritually ill so to counter-attack would only increase his hatred, magnify his attempts to harm you. Therefore visualize him or her. Send forth thoughts of Love and compassion to that person. Send forth a blessing in the name of God. Call for the return of your attacker's soul to goodness and Light, and the cleansing and removal of all evil and hatred. Visualize your attacker's aura and body being irradiated by the holy White Light as a result of your blessing.

8. Salt destroys negativity. If you sense bad vibes in a room or place then sprinkle salt about. It will neutralize all negativity. Basically salt is an incorruptible source for good. Salt nullifies any evil force that it comes into contact with.

9. If you are suffering from unwanted psychic *interference* by a black magician or similar an immediate remedy can be brought about by crossing over running water. Running water has peculiar electrical qualities which break the psychic link between victim and attacker. Cross running water and the attacker will lose your scent and you can make good your escape - this is just as true for victims of psychic attack as it is for animals who are being hunted.

10. Another potent defense is to deny your attackers power. Say forcefully and with conviction, mentally or to his face if he confronts you, *"You have no power over me – your day is done!"*

If you feel that someone is trying to influence you against your better judgment, with or without your knowledge, then refuse to accept his suggestions and declare that he cannot achieve his evil aims. This will return his evil force back upon himself.

11. If anyone tries to dominate you by staring intensely into your eyes do not return eye to eye contact. Instead concentrate your gaze at the spot just above the top of the nose between the inner ends of the eyebrows. Also mentally auto-suggest to yourself that you *will not* be dominated, unduly influenced or hypnotized by anyone. Better still walk away!

12. Ferns, ivies and palms are all useful plants to have around. Not only do they make attractive houseplants, but they also have protective properties. They drive away evil and negativity (especially ferns and ivies) and they emanate uplifting vibrations. It is said that no evil spells can take effect where a cyclamen grows. It is also said that if kept in a bedroom the cyclamen will ward off negativity and protect you while you sleep.

13. Repeating the Lord's Prayer, the 23rd Psalm and especially the very powerful 91st Psalm is a potent aid against evil and misfortune.

14. Jewelry made of silver is the best sort to wear. Silver is a protective metal which reflects negativity away from the wearer.

15. If you cannot keep your mind off someone you do not like; if you have several dreams about a person on consecutive nights; if you sense a person's presence about you late at night; if you find yourself beginning to agree with someone that you previously

distinctively disagreed with; if you have a general feeling of being under someone's spell, then it could be that the person is attempting black magic or sorcery on you to influence you - especially if they have an interest in the supernatural. But there is a solution. Unknown to most people eggs have the ability to absorb evil energy. The following is an exercise involving eggs which is completely ethical, moral and safe to use:

Obtain a fresh egg and wash it in cold running water. Then dry the egg with a clean cloth. Next get a soft tipped pen or pencil and inscribe your name on the egg. Place the egg by your bed, at the pillow end. Place it on a table or chair so that it is the same level as your head when you sleep and leave it for a week.

When the week is up remove the egg, take it to the bathroom, smash it in the lavatory bowl and flush it away. Repeat the exercise for as long as you see fit.

If the egg cracks or breaks before the week is through remove it immediately - don't handle it, use a scoop of some sort - flush it away. Get another egg and start the process again.

Note A: The egg will absorb and store any evil energy that enters your room - whether this is general negativity or evil psychic energy specifically aimed at you. If the egg breaks either it is full of negativity - or has simply gone bad!

16. At dawn, or thereabouts, go out into your garden and walk barefoot in the dewy grass. You will absorb the earth's magnetism which is drawn to the surface by the rising sun. This is a tremendous exercise to do if you wish to restore and strengthen nerves and bodily defenses.

17. For a refreshing nights rest, just before you go to sleep visualize the four Archangels - Auriel, Gabriel, Michael and Raphael - standing guard over you, one at each corner of your bed. Visualize too an aura of White Light surrounding your bed; the two forming an impenetrable force-field of Love, protecting you from all evil and misfortune.

18. Harm no one, neither man or beast. Be good and kind to all. Cause no sorrow, pain or suffering to any living thing, not even the tiniest of insects. Become a vegetarian, or better still a vegan as meat pollutes the soul and poisons the body.

    If you take care of your fellow man and the lesser brethren in their need, the Higher Forces will assuredly take care of you and yours.

19. If you suspect someone of psychically attacking you make sure that they don't get hold of anything personal belonging to you. Do not lend them anything and keep the full date of your birth a secret from them.

Also avoid solitude, drugs and alcohol. Take plenty of sunshine. Seek help from either an experienced genuine Light Worker, psychic practitioner or a clergyman.

20. In New York about thirty plus years ago a number of men, for some reason or other, fell afoul of a Voodoo magician. Being an evil character he set out to destroy them.

He made Voodoo dolls of each of them and carried out nightly pin-sticking rituals on the dolls. He informed the men of his actions and, not unnaturally, they were extremely frightened.

Through a combination of fear and evil psychic energy their health steadily deteriorated, to a point where they were quite literally dying. A kindly wise man heard of their plight and offered to travel to the magician to reason with him.

He visited the Voodooist and on his return he informed them the curse had been lifted and the dolls destroyed. The men immediately felt better and, within days they recovered.

The extraordinary thing was that the Voodooist had refused to end the attack. It was, therefore, equally as destructive when they were recovering as when they were dying. The wise man used psychology to save the men's lives.

This story goes to show the terrible self-destructive damage generated by fear. It also goes to show the great power of the mind when rightly motivated and directed.

21. If you believe someone is trying to psychically influence you there is a simple defensive technique.

    Naturally any psychic attack is going to come via the victim's psychic centers. Therefore, to block the attack, the centers need to be closed down. There is one simple way to do this - eating!

    When there is food in the stomach the psychic centers are automatically closed down and all the body's energy is directed into the digestion and assimilation of the food and its nutrients.

    For an effective force of psychic energy to enter or leave the body the stomach needs to be empty. This is the reason genuine spiritual healers always fast before attempting a healing.

22. If you are afraid of the possibility of someone physically attacking or harming you, call on Archangel Michael to come down with his mighty sword, shielding and protecting you from harm. This is particularly good if you are in a bad neighborhood at night or someplace unfamiliar.

Whether under psychic or physical attack, always center your thoughts on God. It is immeasurably more difficult for a black magician to get a psychic *grip* on a truly religious person, regardless of any psychic self-defense technique being employed.

The person of genuine high consciousness is immune to psychic attack, their aura being imbued with such a powerful force field of Light that no malefic energy can penetrate it.

14

Protective Herbs

Herbs can be worn on the body, carried in a pouch or medicine bad, sprinkled around the house, burned as incense, bathed in or simmered in a pot. Following is a list of herbs that protect against invasion and psychic attack that you may want to consider using.

Agrimony: Acts as a deflective shield and sends bad vibrations back to their source.

Angelica: A highly protective herb said to summon the angels. In its tea form, it can be sprinkled in a few corners of a house to keep evil away.

Anise: Raises vibrations to the highest possible psychic level. Good for bringing about changes in attitude and refocusing thoughts.

Stuffed inside a pillow, it is said to keep away .nightmares that could be caused by astral attack.

Asafetida: One of the foulest smelling and strongest of the protective herbs. Traditionally it was used in exorcism and purification rituals to drive away evil and destroy manifestations.

Bay Leaves: Powerful protective herb used for banishing evil spirits and ghosts.

Betony: A banishing herb used for removing negative energy.

Birdweed: Used in protection to stop an astral attack, and as the rope in binding rituals.

Blueberry: Used for protection as it guards against deception and secrecy.

Camphor: Used to cleanse and banish all forms of psychic aggression.

Capsicum (Cayenne Pepper): Used to reverse evil and return it to the sender.

Cedar: Protects mediums and channels from psychic attack while the Third Eye is open. In some cultures, the oil is used to anoint the Third Eye before meditation.

Deer's Tongue: Used to diagnose possession and reveal the presence of bad energy.

Dragon's Blood: Used in rituals for psychic power and astral protection.

Elm bark: Eliminates slander, gossip, criticism and bad thought forms.

Eucalyptus: Used to cleanse an environment of bad spirits.

Fennel: Used to remove spells.

Garlic: Absorbs negativity, Malefic psychic energy and evil entities. This is why vampires are terrified of garlic! The vampire is *sucked* into the garlic clove and ensnared. To clear an evil or bad psychic atmosphere, strew garlic about the place. Garlic will remove negative thought forms.

Geranium: Banishes negativity and gloomy vibes. Very protective. Used to heal the aura of rips and tears due to astral attack.

Hawthorn: Used for protection, purification and banishing rituals.

Hazel: Used to put a damper on envy, jealousy and resentment.

Heather: Protects against elemental spirits.

Hyacinth: Used to replace negative vibes with positive ones.

Lavender: Cleanses, protects and shields from bad vibrations and negativity, particularly from an ex-lover.

Lemon Verbena: Converts negative energy into positive. Cleanses negative vibrations.

Lilly of the Valley: Used for calming spirits and blessing an environment.

Marjoram: Used for protecting a family or a house from evil spirits and bad luck in general.

Mistletoe: Used since ancient times for protection.

Motherwort : Used for astral protection.

Myrtle: Hung on front doors for protection against psychic aggression.

Onion: Without doubt the most powerful in our fight against evil are those of the onion family. Place halved onions in rooms to absorb diseases and illnesses. Discard the onions next day. For nightly protection from bad vibes and negative forces, place two onions, cut in half and place them in each corner of your bedroom, or at the corners of your bed. They will absorb all the negativity that enters the room. In the morning gather them up and burn them.

Pennyroyal: Cleanses and protects the family home and clears away spirits that might be causing family arguments.

Pine: Repairs shattered auras, clears negative thought forms and aids channels in focusing.

Rosemary: The herb Rosemary is a sacred plant. Wearing oil of Rosemary as a general perfume will afford you divine protection and it will help create a protective force field around your aura to repel evil influences. It is also used for purification and protection of the home.

Rue: Highly protective. Guards against negative energies and forces stagnant energy to move in a positive direction. Thaws frozen energy and breaks binding spells.

St. John's Wort: Rapidly reverses animosity between people. Grounds and dispels negative energies.

Sandalwood: Used to heighten spiritual vibrations, to cleanse, heal and protect.

Sassafras: Used to free you of another's power over you.

Slippery Elm: Protects against gossip or slander.

Snakeroot: Use when you want to be rid of a person or thing. Disconnects individuals at the astral level.

Thyme: Raises vibrations to a higher level and encourages the practical application of spiritual principles in life. Used for protection against psychic invasion and psychic vampires.

Vetivert (khus khus): Used for removal of bad spirits and refocusing of the Third Eye. Replaces negative thought forms with positive ones.

15

Quick & Easy Protection

No matter how good you are a psychic protection, sometimes you'll need to give yourself a little boost. Certain situations or people call for special measures. If you practice these methods regularly, they'll become automatic and a way of life. Always keep in mind, "Fear opens the way, so banish the fear!"

Bad Vibes, Negative Emotions
- ~ fold your arms across your solar plexus, cross your ankles
- ~ hold up a shield or mirror (physical or visualized)
- ~ jump into a bright, beautiful column of light
- ~ carry an Apache Tear (black obsidian) in your pocket
- ~ play appropriate music
- ~ crystallize your aura
- ~ smudge yourself with sage
- ~ carry a protective crystal (Black Tourmaline, turquoise, rose quartz)

- stand under a shower, visualizing that the water is cleaning and clearing your aura

Dark or Dangerous Places
- cloak your light with a black all-enveloping cloak to "make you dim"
- call on your guardian or power animal to accompany you
- carry a mental sword of protection
- cross yourself

To Ward-off an Attack
- electrify the outer edges of your aura
- place a mental mirror in front of the attacker
- wear a Black Tourmaline
- mentally place the attacker in a witches jar
- call on your guardian or power animal to come to your defense

Psychic Vampirism
- cross your arms and ankles
- use a psychic laser (or selenite) to cut the connection
- wear a cross
- carry garlic
- strengthen your aura
- wear protective crystals

Common Sense Guidelines
- Keep your protection up at all times, unless absolutely safe.
- Know your guide, guardian and protector.
- Know yourself.
- Remember: alcohol, drugs and psychic work do not mix.

- Only work psychically when in the best of physical, mental, emotional and psychic health.
- Always come fully back into your body and the present moment after any kind of meditation, healing, channeling, or astral travelling.
- Remember that like attracts like, work on the highest vibration for the best motives and results.
- Don't meditate in a place or in the presence of people with "bad vibes.
- ***Don't meddle with what you don't fully understand.***

15

Basic Spell-Crafting for Protection

We've told you about how to work with your thoughts, visualization, bringing-in guides, creating sacred space… now it's time for a little info on spells. It seems like most everyone has done spells at one time or another, whether they practice Wicca or not. These are all over the internet for everyone to see or use.

We don't necessarily condone spells, but if you decide that a spell is the ONLY way to protect yourself from someone, just keep in mind about the Laws of Return, the Rule of 3, and our old friend Karma. Essentially, **whatever you do to another will come back to you, so make certain of your decision to cast a spell against someone.**

Witch's Jar

This is an easy spell to create and it doesn't harm anyone… unless they cross boundaries to harm you in some way. The purpose of a Witch's Jar is to have as many pointy, sharp things packed into the jar as possible. When someone energetically starts to 'come after you' they will feel the prick of the sharp objects in the jar and will retreat. Most people bury this jar at their front door or at the front door of their business.

1. Take a glass jar and wash it out really well.
2. Fill the jar with sharp objects: nails, wire, pins, needles, razor blades, whatever you can think of that's sharp to the touch.
3. Once your jar is full, place your DNA inside, hair, nail clippings, blood, urine, whatever you're up to adding to the mix.
4. Top the jar off with an egg and place the lid on, sealing it with candlewax.
5. Bury the jar close-by, either near your home, office – just so long as it won't be disturbed.
6. As you are burying your jar, visualize anyone who seeks to harm you as pricking their fingers on the sharp objects placed in the jar and pulling away. Many people believe that you need to have an incantation while placing this in the ground however I sent a prayer up to my Angels for protection when I did mine.

Freezing Your Enemy

This is the easiest spell I know of. If someone in particular is doing something specific to harm you, (i.e. trashing your reputation, messing with your business, chasing your clients away or spreading rumors about you), you can 'freeze' them and prevent them from further harming you.

1. Write on a piece of paper the name of the person harming you and what they're doing to you. Go into some detail, although it's not necessary to write more than just a few sentences.
2. Open a brand new bottle of water (16 oz is fine). Roll the paper up and place it inside the full water bottle.
3. Place this bottle in the freezer, so that it will 'freeze' the person and their negative actions in place. Make sure that this bottle isn't disturbed or used by anyone, as this might have an effect on them, too.

Mirror Image

Unfortunately there are ugly people in the world who spread rumors about us, talk negatively about us, try to harm our reputation, you name it. When reason and conversation just won't work, it's time to take more serious measures to protect yourself. I believe that this could have karmic implications, so you'd better make sure that you're in the right and prepared for consequences if you decide to do it.

1. Get two small mirrors from the craft store.

2. Either take a business card of the person, their photo or write their name and basic information on a piece of paper.
3. Place the paper between the mirrors so that the reflective surfaces face each other.
4. Wrap the mirrors with red string, yarn or ribbon – declaring that you are binding this person from speaking ill about you or attacking you publically. Once you have made 13 wraps on the mirrors, finish with tying three knots.
5. Seal the edge of the mirrors, as well as the binding string with candlewax.
6. You can place this in the place where it's most appropriate, either in the office (inside a planter), at home near the front door, wherever you feel is best and it will be undisturbed.
7. Once the problem is resolved, destroy the mirrors.

To Remove An Unwelcome Entity

Speak directly to the entity, or in the room most affected, saying:

> *It is time to leave here; all is well.*
> *There is nothing here for you now, You must be gone*
> *Go now, go ~ complete your passing,*
> *Go, and with our blessing fare well. Farewell.*

Remove everything of the previous occupant ~ writing and photos in particular.

If there is anything you wish to keep, purify it with salt or incense, saying:

TERI VAN HORN

With this I purify you of the past
Of hurt and memories
Keeping only Love

Shield of Protection

This is something that I've used for quite a while & it's worked great!
1. Draw a large diagram of the shield for protection, by hand. Ideally this is the size of a regular sheet of paper. This must be done in your own hand, making copies doesn't work for this.
2. Once your shield is drawn, locate a space in your home or office to place it, where it will not be interrupted or moved. Make certain that when you find the idea location for your grid, you place the small circles facing north.
3. On the X in the center, place a small glass bottle, with gold and your DNA (saliva on a piece of cotton is fine), seal this bottle with a cork.

Once you place the bottle on the grid, say a brief prayer, asking for protection from harm and leave it in place.

About a year ago, I had someone who had placed a spell on my business, so I used four of these grids – one for each corner of the house. Between that and saying prayers of protection and invocations, I was able to break the spell within three days.

Shield of Protection

ABOUT THE AUTHOR

Teri and her husband, William, live on a small ranch in Texas with their nine horses, four dogs and three doves. She spends her free time working with the animals and her herb garden.

Teri provides healing sessions both in person and through distant healing, in addition to intuitive readings. She teaches workshops on Reiki, working with crystals, psychic protection and manifesting.

You can reach Teri thru her website at
www.healinglightonline.com

Printed in the USA
CPSIA information can be obtained
at www.ICGtesting.com
LVHW051811091224
798715LV00032B/264